BLACKS IN THE MARINE CORPS

By
Henry I. Shaw, Jr.
and
Ralph W. Donnelly

HISTORY AND MUSEUMS DIVISION
HEADQUARTERS, U.S. MARINE CORPS
WASHINGTON, D.C.

REPRINTED 2002

FOREWORD

When this monograph was published almost 30 years ago, then History and Museums Director Brigadier General Edwin H. Simmons wrote: "Today's generation of Marines serve in a fully integrated Corps where blacks constitute almost one-fifth of our strength. Black officers, noncommissioned officers, and privates are omnipresent, their service so normal a part of Marine life that it escapes special notice. The fact that this was not always so and that as little as 34 years ago [in 1941] there were no black Marines deserves explanation." This statement holds true for this edition of *Blacks in the Marine Corps*, which has already gone through several previous reprintings.

What has occurred since the first edition of *Blacks in the Marine Corps* has been considerable scholarship and additional writing on the subject that deserve mention to a new generation of readers, both in and outside the Corps. First and foremost is Morris J. MacGregor, Jr.'s *Integration of the Armed Forces 1940-1965* (Washington, D.C.: U.S. Army Center of Military History, 1981) that documents the Armed Forces efforts as part of the Defense Studies Series. The volume is an excellent history of a social topic often difficult for Service historical offices to deal with.

Two other more recent Marine Corps studies include Bernard C. Nalty's *The Right to Fight: African-American Marines in World War II* (Washington, D.C.: History and Museums Division, 1995) and Colonel Alphonse G. Davis' *Pride, Progress, and Propects: The Marine Corp's Efforts to Increase the Presence of African-American Officers, 1970-1995* (Washington, D.C.: History and Museums Division, 2000). One a commemorative publication, the other an occasional paper, they both add new insights and research to the subject building upon Henry I. Shaw, Jr. and Ralph W. Donnelly's initial effort.

The continued interest and success of Donnelly and Shaw's narrative is one reason to continue to make it available. Equally important is the story of the Marine Corps' evolution as an institution that draws strength from the diversity of American society. The complete integration of the Corps was not a single event in the past, but a series of individual and group contributions towards a not always common goal. The success of this effort is measured in today's opportunity for an equal right to serve regardless of race, color, or creed. This is a story that parallels the nation's history.

John W. Ripley
Colonel, U.S. Marine Corps, Retired
Director of Marine Corps History and Museums Division

PREFACE

This has been a difficult history to research. The records of black Marine units are sparse; the administrative correspondence concerning blacks in the Marine Corps is equally scanty. One lucky find was a file of correspondence relating to the efforts to find a place for black Marine barracks detachments in the late 1940s. It came to light as the result of the research efforts of Mr. Morris J. MacGregor of the Army's Center of Military History, who is writing a history of blacks in the Armed Forces for the Department of Defense. A similar unexpected find was several folders of statistical data on black Marines in the 40s and 50s which had been relegated to the back of someone's file drawer in the Manpower Department and happily rediscovered by a person who recognized its historical worth.

The basic information compiled on World War II Marines was gained by a painstaking extraction of data from the monthly muster rolls of black Marine units. The Reference Section of the History and Museums Division has maintained subject files over the years consisting of pertinent newspaper clippings, extracts from official documents, copies of answers of public and official queries, and other valuable miscellaneous pieces of information. Those files pertaining to black Marines were used extensively but with care as to the authenticity of the sources. An assemblage of official documents relating to blacks in the Marine Corps, maintained by the then Personnel Department, and later by the Commandant's Special Assistant on Minority Affairs, was turned over to the Reference Section at the start of the writing of the history.

All apparently pertinent published sources were consulted, but it was soon discovered that very little has been written about black Marines and much of that which has been available is inaccurate. The Camp Lejeune newspaper was read, page by page, from 1942 until 1950 to uncover news of the men of Montford Point. Surprisingly little was published in the way of news stories specifically concerned with black Marines, but the columnists and photographers unwittingly provided a mine of information. A summary history of black Marines which had been prepared in the Historical Branch in 1946, as later enlarged upon by Lieutenant Colonel Kenneth H. Berthoud, Jr., who also added a history of black officers, proved very useful. Colonel Berthoud himself was even more useful as a source of information in his conversations with both authors.

When most of the documentary research had been completed, Mr. Donnelly wrote a first draft of this history. It provided the backbone for much of what is now printed, but it was obvious that more information than could be culled from official sources was needed. To fill the gaps, Mr. Shaw conducted a number of interviews in the summer of 1972 with serving black officers and enlisted men and with black veterans. Key interviews in this series were those with Assistant Secretary of the Navy James E. Johnson, then-Lieutenant Colonel Frank E. Petersen, Jr., Sergeant Major Edgar R. Huff, and retired Sergeant Major Gilbert H. "Hashmark" Johnson. Through the good offices of the Montford Point Marine Association (MMPA), Mr. Shaw was able to hold extensive discussions, both informally and on tape, with members attending the association's 1972 annual meeting. There he benefitted greatly from an extended talk with retired Master Gunnery Sergeant Brooks E. Gray, Jr., first President of the MMPA. Taped interviews were conducted with Marine veterans Herman Darden, Jr., Obie Hall, Alex Johnson, Robert D. Little, and Norman Sneed.

Once the rewrite of the narrative had started, a chance visit from an old friend, Master Gunnery Sergeant Frederick H. Clayton, who had been a classification specialist at Montford Point and with both the 51st and 52d Defense Battalions, provided the answers to several baffling questions. Throughout the writing of the final version of the history, Majors Edward L. Green and Solomon P. Hill were ever ready to provide advice, information, and constructive criticism. Three civilian employees of Headquarters Marine Corps, Joseph H. Carpenter, Charles H. Doom, and David C. Hendricks, all World War II veterans of Montford Point, were particularly helpful in providing background information on personalities and events and in clearing up disputed points about the service of black Marines.

A number of knowledgeable individuals were asked to review the final draft manuscript. The majority of their valuable comments have been incorporated in the text. Active duty reviewers included Colonels Berthoud and Petersen, Majors Green and Hill, and Gunnery Sergeant Roy G. Johnson. Retired and former Marines who read the manuscript included Secretary Johnson, Sergeant Major Huff, Master Gunnery Sergeant Clayton, Mr. Carpenter, and Mr. Hendricks. Dr. Robert Humphrey of the USMC Human Relations Institute at San Diego had the text reviewed by "my best two black advisors in the Corps" and provided their comments. Dr. Charles W. Simmons, Head of the History and Geography Department at Norfolk State College and former sergeant major of the 51st Defense Battalion, was particularly helpful in his review. Mr. MacGregor, drawing on his considerable background in recent black military history, furnished many useful and constructive comments. All members of the 1973–74 Commandant's Advisory Committee on Marine Corps History read and critiqued the manuscript including Major General Donald M. Weller, USMC (Retired), Chairman, Major General Norman J. Anderson, USMC (Retired), Colonel Frederick S. Aldridge, USMC (Retired), Dr. Gordon A. Craig, Dr. Philip K. Lundeberg, and Mr. Robert L. Sherrod.

The editorial review of the manuscript was made by Brigadier General Edwin H. Simmons, Director of Marine Corps History and Museums, and Colonel Herbert M. Hart, Deputy Director for Marine Corps History. The typing of the manuscript through its various drafts was the responsibility in succession of Miss Cynthia L. Brown, Lance Corporal Carl W. Rice, and Miss Catherine A. Stoll. Miss Stoll and PFC Denise L. Alexander prepared the index for the printer. The maps, charts, and cover copy for the history were prepared by Staff Sergeant Paul A. Lloyd. Unless otherwise noted, official Department of Defense photographs were used throughout the text.

RALPH W. DONNELLY

HENRY I. SHAW, JR.

TABLE OF CONTENTS

INTRODUCTION

Prior to President Harry Truman's 1948 declaration of intent to end segregation in the U.S. Armed Forces, blacks who served most often did so in segregated units or under a quota system designed to limit their number. In time of war, the need for men usually required the recruitment or drafting of blacks: in peacetime the number of black servicemen dwindled. In large part, the situation of blacks in uniform was a reflection of their status in society, particularly that part of American society which practiced racial segregation and discrimination.

During the American Revolution blacks served in small numbers in both the Continental and state navies and armies. According to surviving muster and pay rolls, there were at least three blacks in the ranks of the Continental Marines and ten others who served as Marines on ships of the Connecticut, Massachusetts, and Pennsylvania navies.[1] It is probable that more blacks served as Marines in the Revolution who were not identified as such in the rolls. The first recorded black Marine in the Continental service was John Martin or "Keto," a slave of William Marshall of Wilmington, Delaware, who was recruited without Marshall's knowledge or permission by Marine Captain Miles Pennington in April 1776. Martin served on board the Continental brig *Reprisal* until October 1777 when the ship foundered off the Newfoundland Banks. All of her crew except the cook were lost.[2]

On 27 August 1776, Isaac Walker, identified on the rolls as a Negro, was enlisted in Captain Robert Mullan's company of Continental Marines in Philadelphia, and on 1 October, a recruit listed simply as "Orange . . . Negro" was enrolled. Both of these men were still on the company payroll as of 1 April 1777.[3] It is quite possible that they served with Mullan's unit in the Second Battle of Trenton (Assunpink Creek) on 2 January 1777 and in the Battle of Princeton the following day.

Those few black men who have been identified as Marines from surviving Revolutionary War rosters were pioneers who were not followed by others of their race until 1 June 1942. The Continental Marines went out of existence within a year after the Treaty of Paris was signed on 11 April 1783. When Congress conditionally authorized the construction of six frigates for a new Navy in 1794, Marine guards were part of the planned ships' complements. In 1797, after the completion of three of the frigates, *Constitution, Constellation,* and *United States*, was authorized, Marines were actually enlisted. The Secretary of War, who also supervised the Navy, on 16 March 1798 prescribed a set of rules governing the enrollment of Marines for the *Constellation* which provided that "No Negro, Mulatto or Indian to be enlisted. . . ."[4]

These regulations prohibiting the enlistment of Negroes were continued when Congress, on 11 July 1798, reestablished a separate Marine Corps with a major in command. The new Commandant, Major William Ward Burrows, was explicit on the subject in his instructions to his recruiting officers. To Lieutenant John Hall at Charleston, South Carolina, he wrote:

> You may enlist . . . as many Drummers and Fifers as possible, I do not care what Country the D & Fifers are of but you must be careful not to enlist more Foreigners than as one to three natives. You can make use of Blacks and Mulattoes while you recruit, but you cannot enlist them.[5]

The regulations for recruiting Marines were much more selective than those for seamen because of the reliance on the small guards on board ship to maintain discipline, prevent mutinies, and give a military tone to men-of-war. This situation was, in part, a carry over from the experience of British Marines, about whom the observation had been made a hundred years earlier:

> It may be added to what has been said of the usefulness of the said [Marine] Regimt that the whole body of seamen on board the Fleet, being a loose collection of undisciplined people, and (as experience shows) sufficiently inclined to mutiny, the Marine Regimts will be a powerful check to their disorders, and will be able to prevent the disasterous consequences that may thence result to their Mats [Majesties] service.[6]

Certainly those instrumental in recreating the American Navy had before them the spectacle and lesson of the British Navy's Spithead and Nore mutinies of April and May 1797 and the part played by Marines in their suppression.

There is no known record of black Marines serving in the various wars of the 19th Century. The Navy did frequently enlist blacks as seamen, so much so that at one time in 1839 the Secretary of the Navy issued a directive that no more than five percent of enlistees could be blacks.[7] Thousands of blacks served in the Federal Army and Navy during the Civil War and some continued to serve thereafter—in the Army's case in two black infantry and two black cavalry regiments which fought the Indians on the western frontier.

Mixed crews with blacks in all ratings remained a feature of the Navy up until World War I, when the majority of black volunteers were assigned to the Messman Branch. Following the war, black recruitment in the Navy ceased for more than a decade and when it resumed in 1932, blacks were again only enlisted in the Messman Branch.[8] The Army used blacks in segregated units in World War I and continued the practice following the war. At the onset of American involvement in World War II, the segregation of blacks in the Armed Forces continued. Black Army volunteers and draftees were assigned to all-black units. The Navy restricted its black volunteers to steward duty and the Marine Corps accepted no blacks at all.

CHAPTER 1

A CHOSEN FEW

The door was opened for blacks to serve in all branches of the Armed Forces on 25 June 1941 when President Franklin D. Roosevelt issued Executive Order No. 8802 establishing the Fair Employment Practices Commission with this statement:

> In affirming the policy of full participation in the defense program by all persons regardless of color, race, creed, or national origin, and directing certain action in furtherance of said policy . . . all departments of the government, including the Armed Forces, shall lead the way in erasing discrimination over color or race.[1]

Major General Commandant Thomas Holcomb appointed Brigadier General Thomas E. Watson to represent the Marine Corps on the newly established commission, and the Corps took preliminary steps to comply with the President's Executive Order. There is no question but that the order was unpopular at Headquarters Marine Corps. Faced with the necessity of expanding the Corps to meet the threatening war situation, few, if any, of the Marine leaders were interested in injecting a new element into the training picture. There was serious doubt that blacks would meet the high standards of the Marine Corps. Once war had broken out, this opposition stiffened. The Commandant, in testimony before the General Board of the Navy on 23 January 1942, indicated that it had long been his considered opinion that "there would be a definite loss of efficiency in the Marine Corps if we have to take Negroes . . . ."[2]

General Holcomb also indicated that the Marine Corps did not have the facilities or trained personnel to handle all the whites who wanted to join after Pearl Harbor. If there were to be black Marine units, he noted that he could use only "the best type of officer on this project, because it will take a great deal of character and technique to make the thing a success, and if it is forced upon us we must make it a success."[3] The need for experienced noncommissioned officers (NCOs) in training blacks was equally acute and the Commandant felt that "they simply can not be spared if we are going to be ready for immediate service with the fleet."[4] Concluding his remarks, he said, "the Negro race has every opportunity now to satisfy its aspirations for combat, in the Army—a very much larger organization than the Navy or Marine Corps—and their desire to enter the naval service is largely, I think, to break into a club that doesn't want them."[5]

Regardless of the Commandant's private protests, the pressure was on from the White House and from other public sources to get on with the enlistment of blacks for general duty in the Navy and Marine Corps. Wendell L. Wilkie, the titular head of the Republican Party, in a speech delivered at the Freedom House inaugural dinner on 19 March 1942, described the Navy's "racial bias" in excluding blacks from enlisting except as mess attendants as a "mockery." He challenged, "Are we always as alert to practice [democracy] here at home as we are to proclaim it abroad?"[6]

The Administration's answer, delivered by Secretary of the Navy Frank Knox on 7 April, was that the Navy, Coast Guard, and Marine Corps would soon accept blacks for enlistment for general service in active duty reserve components. Actual recruitment would begin when suitable training sites were established.[7] Secretary Knox's statement was followed on 20 May by an announcement from the Navy Department that on 1 June the Navy would begin recruiting 1,000 blacks a month for shore and high seas service and that during June and July a complete battalion of 900 blacks would be formed by the Marine Corps.[8]

This was to be a new experience for the Marine Corps. One officer recalled:

> . . . when the colored came in, we had the appropriations and the authority, and we could have gotten 40,000 white people. It just scared us to death when the colored were put on it. I went over to Selective Service and saw General Hershey, and he turned me

over to a lieutenant colonel [Campbell C. Johnson?]—
that was in April—and he was one grand person. I
told him, "Eleanor [Mrs. Roosevelt] says we gotta take
in Negroes, and we are just scared to death: we've
never had any in; we don't know how to handle them:
we are afraid of them." He said, "I'll do my best to
help you get good ones. I'll get the word around that if
you want to die young, join the Marines. So anybody
that joins [has] got to be pretty good!" And it was the
truth. We got some awfully good Negroes.[9]

The Beginnings

In the course of a study prepared on the
possible uses of blacks in the Marine Corps by
Brigadier General Keller E. Rockey, Director
of the Division of Plans and Policies, the possibility that they might be employed in a
messmen's branch, similar to the Navy's, was
considered, but the Corps at that time did not
have such a branch. Strong doubts were expressed that blacks could serve successfully in
combat units, citing the Army's experience that
the General Classification Test scores of the
majority of black recruits showed low levels of
learning aptitude.[10] The Marine Corps actually
had little choice in the matter. The die had
been cast. There would be blacks in the Marine
Corps and some at least would serve in combat
units. The initial vehicle for that service would
be a composite defense battalion, a unit containing seacoast artillery, antiaircraft artillery,
infantry, and tanks, whose task was overseas
base defense.

Units of this type, their organization always
tailored to their mission, were already deployed overseas and had seen combat. Outnumbered elements of the 1st Defense Battalion had gallantly defended Wake Island from
invading Japanese. Other units of the 1st on
Johnson and Palmyra and of the 3d and 6th
Battalions on Midway had engaged enemy
ships and planes with seacoast defense and antiaircraft guns.[11]

As General Holcomb had pointed out to the
General Board, the selection of an officer to
head the black unit, in fact to oversee all black
Marine training, was crucial. The choice was a
wise and fortunate one. Colonel Samuel A.
Woods, Jr., a native of South Carolina and a
graduate of The Citadel, had some 25 years
experience as an officer, including service in
France in World War I, duty in Cuba, China,
the Dominican Republic, and the Philippines,
and service with the fleet.[12] In addition to a
varied and well rounded career, he had personal qualities that made him a memorable

Colonel Samuel A. Woods, Jr., first Commanding Officer, 51st
Composite Defense Battalion and Montford Point Camp. (USMC
Photo 9511).

man to the first black Marines. Almost univer-
sally they speak of him with respect and affec-
tion. In the words of one black NCO who
served closely with him, his most outstanding
quality was "his absolute fairness. He would
throw the book at you if you had it coming, but
he would certainly give you an opportunity to
prove yourself."[13]

Colonel Woods, basing his findings upon a
General Board report to Secretary Knox of 20
March, presented his plans for the program to
be established for black Marines to General
Rockey on 21 April. He based his concept on a
minimum of 1,000 black reserve recruits to be
equipped as a defense battalion after six
months. Training was to be conducted at
Mumford Point (later renamed Montford
Point) at the Marine Barracks, New River,
North Carolina. The barracks, soon to be
named Camp Lejeune, was already the major
east coast combat training site for Fleet Marine
Force (FMF) units and it would soon be the
only training site for black Marines. The sum
of $750,000 was alloted to construct and en-
large temporary barracks and supporting
facilities for the new camp at Montford Point.

Some of the colonel's plan came to fruition,

other parts were changed to meet the circumstances at Montford Point. Basically, however, a headquarters and service battery and one or more recruit training batteries would be formed as the initial camp complement. The first recruits to report would have cooking experience. It was expected that boot camp and basic training would take 180 days. At the end of this time, the black Marines would receive combat equipment and organize for training as a composite defense battalion. The first appointments of black NCOs would be made at about the same time.

Colonel Woods recognized the battalion's table of organization contained "some ranks which normally require considerable experience and more than 12 years' service to attain." [14] Since the unit was eventually to be composed entirely of black enlisted men and white officers, blacks would have to learn on the job to fill all NCO billets. Promotion was to be governed by length of service, experience, and demonstrated ability, and controlled by changes in the training allowance for the battalion. [15]

Recruiting was to begin on 1 June 1942. Although the public announcement was not made until 20 May, the basic instructions for Marine Corps Recruiting Divisions were sent out in a letter from the Commandant on 15 May. This letter set a quota of 200 recruits each from the Eastern and Central Divisions while the Southern was to furnish 500 of the initial 900 recruits. These men were to be citizens between 17 and 29 years of age, and they were to meet the existing standards for enlistment in the Corps. They were to be enlisted in Class III (c), Marine Corps Reserve, and assigned to inactive duty in a General Service Unit of their Reserve District. Both the service record book and the enlistment contract were to be stamped "Colored." [16]

When recruiting opened on 1 June, the first men to enlist were Alfred Masters and George O. Thompson (1 June), George W. James and John E. L. Tillman (2 June), Leonard L. Burns (3 June), and Edward A. Culp (5 June), all in the 8th Reserve District, headquartered at Pensacola, Florida. On 8 June, James W. Brown in the 3d District (New York) and George L. Glover and David W. Sheppard in the 6th and 7th Districts (Charleston) enlisted. From then on the number on the rolls gradually rose, with the instructions to recruiters that the first men to be sent to Montford Point would be those

who had skills that would help ready the camp for those to follow.

The majority of the recruits were well motivated to join the Marine Corps. One recruit, Edgar R. Huff, from Gadsden, Alabama, who later became the senior sergeant major in the Marine Corps, expressed the feelings of a lot of those first men when he said: "I wanted to be a Marine because I had always heard that the Marine Corps was the toughest outfit going and I felt that I was the toughest going, and so I wanted to be a member of the best organization." [17]

Other recruits, faced with a long delay in reporting to boot camp unless they had qualifications that were needed in the initial camp setup, stretched the truth a little. In Boston, a young black, Obie Hall, who eventually became the first man in the first squad in the first regular recruit platoon organized at Montford Point, told the recruiting sergeant that he could drive a truck. He recalled later, "I could no more drive a truck than a man in the moon, [but] I said, 'I'm a truck driver.'" [18] And as a result he arrived at Montford Point on 2 September 1942.

The original schedule called for about 25 cooks, bakers, and barbers to report to camp on 26 August. The next 100 men were to report on 2–3 September and another 125 or so with miscellaneous qualifications were to arrive on 16–17 September. The middle of each month thereafter was to bring about 200 recruits until the target total of 1,200 men was reached. [19]

The Camp Opens

On 18 August 1942, Headquarters and Service Battery of the 51st Composite Defense Battalion was activated at Montford Point with Colonel Woods as battalion commander. His executive officer and officer in charge of recruit training was Lieutenant Colonel Theodore A. Holdahl, a World War I enlisted man commissioned as a regular officer in 1924, who had served in the Philippines, China, Nicaragua, and British Guiana. [20] Battery strength, all white Marines, was 23 officers and 90 enlisted men, these last soon to be known to black recruits as SES men (Special Enlisted Staff). While there was a sprinkling of experienced officers and warrant officers, the majority of the commissioned strength was second lieutenants not long out of officers' training at

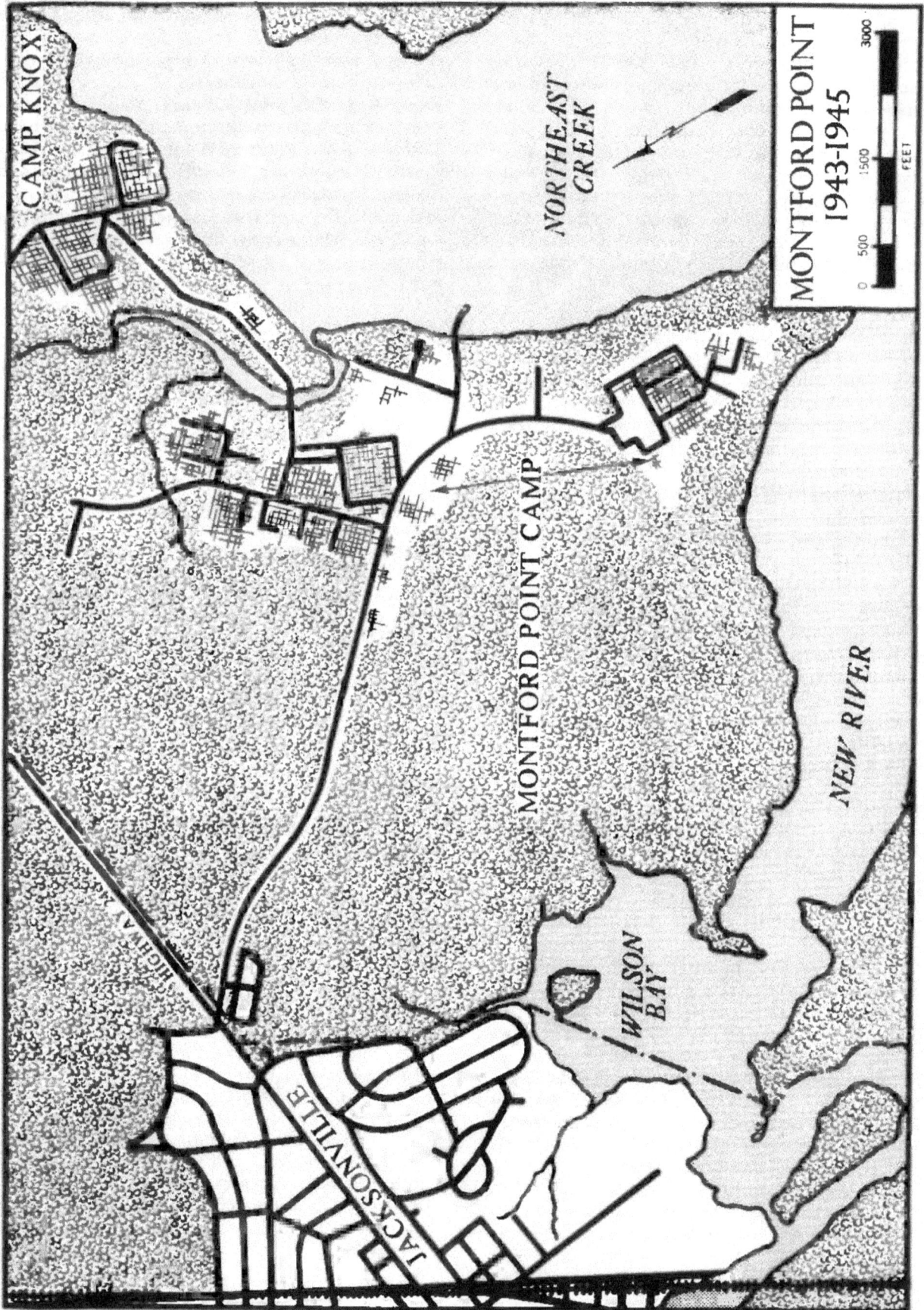

CAMP KNOX

NORTHEAST CREEK

MONTFORD POINT
1943-1945

FEET

MONTFORD POINT CAMP

NEW RIVER

HIGHWAY 24

WILSON BAY

JACKSONVILLE

the Marine Corps Schools, Quantico, Virginia. The staff NCOs, sergeants, and some of the corporals were men with years of experience in the Marine Corps. The few privates first class (PFCs) and privates filled clerical, motor transport, and other camp support billets.

The men chosen to be drill instructors (DIs) were "old line" Marines, men who were to impress the black recruits with their bearing and firmness of manner. In the memory of one of the few recruits who had had prior experience in the Armed Forces, Gilbert H. Johnson, these DIs "set about from the very beginning to get us thoroughly indoctrinated into the habits and the thinking and the actions of the Marine Corps. Discipline seemed to be their lone stock in trade, and they applied it with a vengeance, very much to our later benefit." [21]

On schedule, 13 of the 24 black recruits expected in August arrived at Montford Point on the 26th. The first black private to set foot in the camp was Howard P. Perry of Charlotte, North Carolina. He was joined on that eventful first day by Jerome D. Alcorn, Willie B. Cameron, Otto Cherry, Lawrence S. Cooper, Harold O. Ector, Eddie Lee, Ulysses J. Lucas, Robert S. Parks, Jr., Edward Polin, Jr., Emerson E. Roberts, Gilbert C. Rousan, and James O. Stallworth. The rest of the 23 men who eventually arrived in August came in over the next five days. Battery A of the 51st Composite Defense Battalion was organized on 26 August "as an administrative and tactical unit for the training of recruit platoons," with Second Lieutenant Anthony Caputo as commanding officer. [22]

In September recruit training began in earnest. What Montford Point Marines later called the "Mighty" 1st, 2d, and 3d Recruit Platoons were organized with 40 men in each platoon. Several SES NCOs were assigned to each platoon to give the men experience in handling black recruits; as more men came in in mid-September many of the original DIs were transferred to help form new platoons. This was to be the experience of the first few months, in fact it was not long before exceptional recruits were being singled out and made "Acting Jacks," assistant DIs in their own platoons. This came about partially because of the shortage of white NCOs and equally as well because one purpose of all training at Montford Point was to discover and develop potential black NCOs.

The number of voluntary enlistments of black Marines was not up to the anticipated rate. The requirement for these first recruits to have ability in needed skills was undoubtedly a factor in the slow intake. It became necessary on 9 October to modify the plans for assembling the black personnel of the 51st, and the assignment of experienced SES personnel had to be curtailed in the face of pressure for men for FMF units already deployed in the Pacific. Although it had been anticipated that 1,200 black recruits would be enlisted by the end of October less than 600 were in camp. [23] The Commandant was writing as late as 19 December that "colored personnel will continue to be procured and ordered to the 51st Composite Defense Battalion at the rate of 200 recruits per month until 1,200 is reached." [24]

The camp at this time made an indelible impression on the incoming recruits. Coming off Highway 24 near the small and sleepy town of Jacksonville, a narrow road about a mile long led through a corridor of tall pine trees into a large clearing where there was:

> . . . a headquarters building (#100), a chapel, two warehouses, a theatre building with two wings, which later housed a library, barber shop, [and] classification room on one side and a recreation slop chute [beer hall] on the other, a dispensary building, a mess hall, designated by the recruits as "The Greasy Spoon," quarters and facilities for the SES personnel, a small steam generating plant, a small motor transport compound, a small officers' club, and 120 green prefabricated huts, each designed for billeting 16 men. [25]

Surrounding the open spaces of the main camp area were thick pine forests. Beyond the north forest area was Highway 24, to the south the point of land that gave the area its name thrust into the New River, to the west was the river, Wilson Bay, and the town of Jacksonville, and to the east was Scales Creek, which had notorious areas of quicksand. Across the creek was an old Civilian Conservation Corps (CCC) camp area now partially occupied by a war dog training center. In all there was about 5½ square miles of rugged ground in the original camp site. Mosquitoes abounded, the woods were full of snakes, and bears padded about through the camp, much to the consternation of recruits who saw their tracks when they fell out for morning roll call. There was a lot of bush in the camp area to start off with, but the boots soon cleared it away or wore it away with their incessant drilling.

Part and parcel of this somewhat drab and uninviting encampment was the traditional DI reception the incoming recruits received. The idea at all boot camps, whether white at Parris

Montford Point Camp as it appeared in 1943. In the left center is the mess hall; in right center are the "little green huts" of boot camp. (Photo from Montford Point Pictorial).

Island and San Diego or black at Montford Point, was to knock the new recruit off balance, keep him on the run, hammer at him physically and psychologically day and night, and eventually meld him as an individual into a member of a team, his platoon. There was ample room for the men to believe one DI's statement, "I'm going to make you wish you never had joined this damn Marine Corps." [26]

In point of fact, however, Gilbert Johnson, who had served six years in the Army's black 25th Infantry on the Mexican Border in the 1920s and most of the 1930s as a Navy mess attendant and officers' steward, sagely observed in regard to the white DIs that "the policy was to select the type of individuals who were not against the Negro being a Marine, and had it been otherwise, why I'm afraid that we would have all left the first week. Some of us, probably, the first night." [27]

Johnson, who had been an Officers' Steward 2d Class, had asked to be discharged from the Navy in order to enlist in the Marine Corps as a private. The Commandant and the Secretary

of the Navy concurred in his request; he received his discharge, enlisted in the Marines, and soon became known, once out of boot camp, as "Hashmark" Johnson, because of the prior service stripes that he wore on his sleeves. Due in part to his age, 37, when he reached Montford Point, his considerable service experience, and a serious dedication to making a success of being a Marine, he was destined to become a legend in his own lifetime to the first black Marines, an elder statesman and historian of the Montford Point experience.

But "Hashmark" Johnson was far from the only memorable man who joined in those first few months when volunteers filled the ranks at Montford Point. The recruiters had been selective; there were other men with Army service, John T. Pridgen, who had been a member of the black 10th Cavalry in the late 1930s, and George A. Jackson, who had been an Army lieutenant. Both eventually became drill instructors. There was a host of college graduates and men who had had college training including Charles F. Anderson, a graduate of Morehouse College, who arrived in September and eventually became the first black sergeant major of Montford Point Camp and Charles W. Simmons, a graduate of Alcorn A and M with a masters degree from the University of Illinois, who wound up as sergeant major of the 51st Defense Battalion.[28] The man who was to become the senior bayonet and unarmed combat instructor of black recruits, Arvin L. "Tony" Ghazlo, a former bodyguard and jujitsu instructor from Philadelphia,[29] arrived in October, and the next month saw the man who was to be his principal assistant, Ernest "Judo" Jones, reach Montford Point. Besides teaching the recruits, these two and their assistants were responsible for many memorable exhibitions of unarmed combat techniques.

There were many of those early recruits who became men of note amongst black Marines and, in fact, men of substance in their communities in later life. They were, in general, a select body of young men; the recruiters had tried hard to find and send to Montford Point men with technical, educational, and work backgrounds who had the potential to fill out the various billets of a defense battalion. The call for such specialists could not be completely met, however, and the Commandant was informed in late October that it was "doubtful if even white recruits could be procured with the

Corporal Alvin "Tony" Ghazlo, senior bayonet and unarmed combat instructor at Montford Point, disarms his assistant, Private Ernest "Judo" Jones. (USMC Photo 5334).

qualifications listed . . . ." [30] This racial comparison of relative skills was not as odious as it might seem today, but rather a statement of the prevailing situation in most of the country, where the general education level of blacks was lower than that of whites and the chances for skilled job experience were severely limited for blacks.

The First Graduates

By the end of November 1942, the initial recruit platoons were near the finish of their eight weeks of boot camp. Two weeks preliminary marksmanship training was conducted at Montford Point, culminated by a week of live firing at the Camp Lejeune rifle range near Stone Bay. Since there were as yet no living facilities for blacks at the range, the recruits found themselves trucked to the range before dawn and returned to camp after nightfall. Still, they did well, and the majority of the first 198 men to graduate from boot camp qualified as rifle marksmen or sharpshooters, enabling them to wear their qualification badges proudly on their uniforms. Even more important to the men, the first blacks were qualified to sew rank stripes on their uniforms in November. On the 1st, 16 privates were promoted to private first class and on the 19th, four privates were promoted to assistant cook. Many of the new PFCs had been acting as assistant DIs to the SES NCOs, some had even finished up the training of their platoons as the white DIs were spread thin among newly formed units. Others of the new "one stripers" were slated to take over office duties in existing or planned headquarters, while the newly designated cooks would man the kitchens of the 51st's messhall.

In early December, the new graduates had their first opportunity to go on liberty and poured out the front gate walking down the long road to Jacksonville. Their reception was a rude awakening to the men. The sight of a couple of hundred blacks in Marine green coming into the little town was unnerving to the merchants, and they closed down their stores. Far more disturbing, the bus station and the ticket office were also closed, and the young blacks had seemingly lost their opportunity to leave "J-ville." They had no intention of staying in town, they wanted to get out, to take a bus to Wilmington, Kinston, or New Bern, larger towns with substantial black popu-

lations. In this instance, as in many, Colonel Woods was the champion of the black Marines. He ordered out the 51st's trucks, which took the men to their chosen liberty towns, stayed with them, and brought them back to Montford Point. And he took steps to ensure that the buses were available thereafter to the black Marines. Yet, the actualities of segregation in the South made the use of these buses a sore point with the men at Montford Point. Not only did they have to ride in the back of the bus, they were often arbitrarily denied entrance by the white bus drivers while the buses were filled with white Marines returning from liberty. On a few occasions during the course of the war years, white bus drivers who attempted such arbitrary action found themselves abandoned beside the road while a delighted crew of black Marines returned themselves to Montford Point in the commandeered buses.

With the advent of promotions and liberty came new assignments for the first recruit graduates. The 51st Composite Defense Battalion began to take shape. On 1 December, Rifle Company (Reinforced) of the 51st was organized. But its immediate function belied its name, for it was primarily a schools and training organization for the many specialists needed. Student bandsmen, cooks, clerks, communicators, and truck drivers were among the men who filled its ranks. Some of these individuals were already experienced in their specialties, others had been selected to learn by formal schooling or on-the-job training. Also formed on the 1st was a 155mm gun battery and a 90mm antiaircraft group. On 21 December, a 75mm pack howitzer battery was organized. Remaining behind in Battery A were nine privates and 12 PFCs, six of the latter to serve as DIs and six as battery clerks.

December offered many of the newly minted Marines a chance for a week's furlough; many were home for Christmas or New Year's Day. Their misadventures were many, for their number was still small, and the existence of black Marines was apparently not widely known. In several instances, men were questioned or arrested for impersonating a Marine, but the misunderstandings were usually cleared up in short order.

Expansion Looms

While the 51st Composite Defense Battalion, still the vehicle for handling all black Marines,

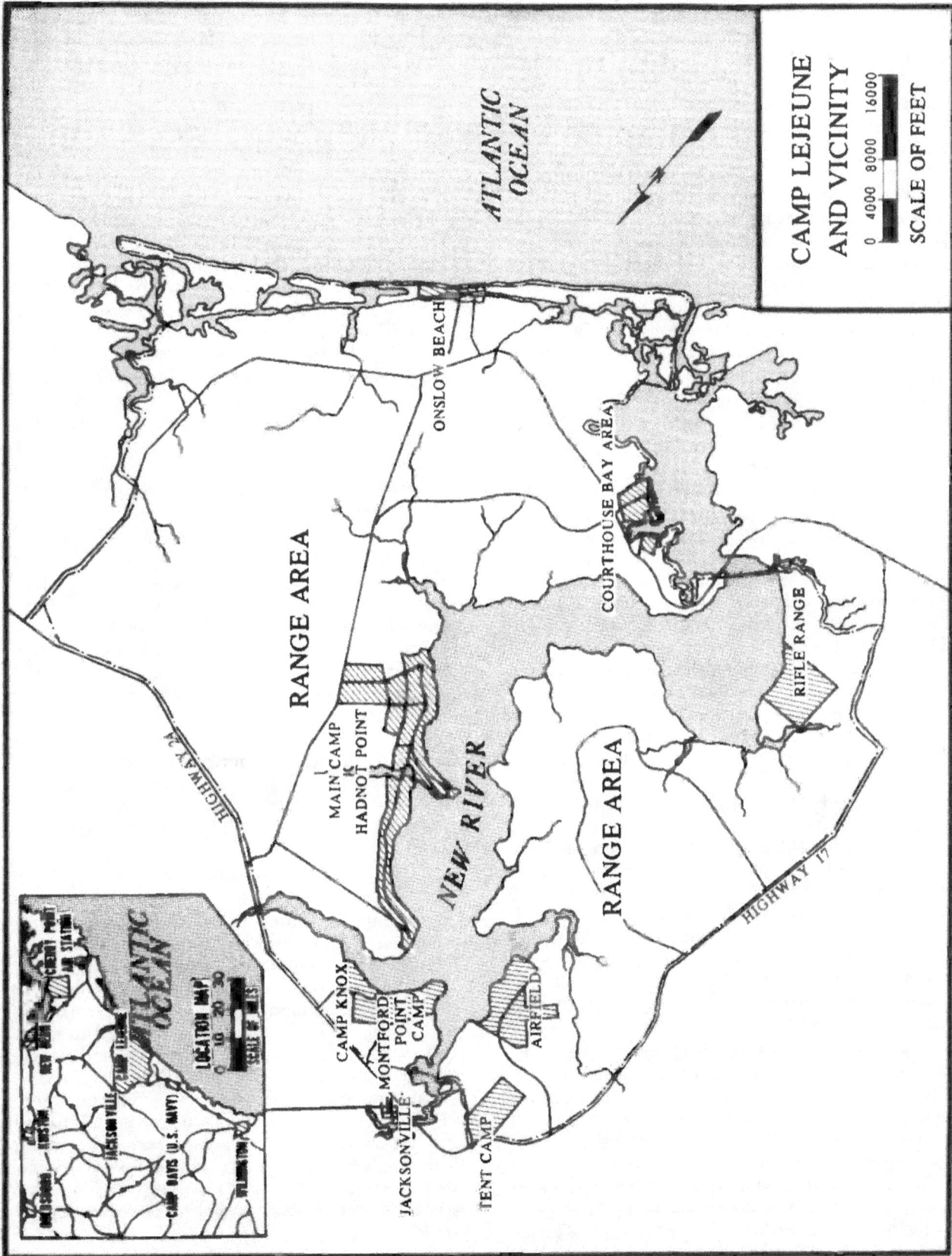

CAMP LEJEUNE
AND VICINITY

SCALE OF FEET

0   4000   8000   16000

ATLANTIC OCEAN

RANGE AREA

RANGE AREA

NEW RIVER

ONSLOW BEACH

COURTHOUSE BAY AREA

RIFLE RANGE

MAIN CAMP
HADNOT POINT

HIGHWAY 24

HIGHWAY 17

CAMP KNOX

MONTFORD POINT CAMP

JACKSONVILLE

TENT CAMP

AIRFIELD

LOCATION MAP

SCALE OF MILES

0   10   20   30

ATLANTIC OCEAN

JACKSONVILLE

CAMP DAVIS (U.S. NAVY)

was in the process of reorganization, there was the prospect of a whole new ball game insofar as blacks in the Marine Corps was concerned. Instead of 1,200 men, one defense battalion and its training base, there were going to be thousands more men arriving at Montford Point.

On 5 December 1942, voluntary enlistments in the Armed Forces were discontinued for all men 18 to 37 years of age, although 17 year olds and, in some instances, those 38 or older could still volunteer for the Navy and Marine Corps. Beginning in January 1943, all men in the 18–37 age group would be inducted into the services through the Selective Service System. To make the call-up equitable, at least 10 percent of those selected would be blacks, a proportion approximating the number of blacks in the U.S. population as a whole.

The Army, which was the principal beneficiary of the stopping of the flow of the volunteers into the other services, was interested in having the Marine Corps concentrate on taking black draftees until it had reached the same percentage of blacks in its ranks that the Army already had. This concept was unacceptable to the Corps, since it would have severely disrupted existing training plans for replacements and new combat units, but there was no arguing with the imposition of an induction quota. Its advent was recognized early in the year's planning and was confirmed in a memorandum of 8 March 1943 from Headquarters Marine Corps to the Chief of Naval Personnel. Since the approved increase between 1 February and 31 December 1943 was 99,000 men, this placed a requirement on the Corps for the acquisition and accommodation of 9,900 blacks. In order to meet this goal, calls were placed with Selective Service for 400 men in February and March, 800 in April, 1,300 in May, and 1,000 men per month thereafter. Any increase in the authorized strength of the Marine Corps would lead to a corresponding increase in the monthly draft calls for black Marines.[31]

Obviously, Montford Point was due for drastic expansion, and the 51st Composite Defense Battalion could not be the vehicle to absorb such numbers. Some of the new men would have the opportunity of becoming officers' stewards, cooks, and messmen, for the Secretary of the Navy on 1 January had authorized the formation of a Messman Branch (eventually Stewards' Branch) in the Marine Corps,

composed entirely of black Marines. Still others of the incoming thousands would serve in a second defense battalion that was contemplated as a follow on to the 51st. But most of the new recruits, in fact the majority of World War II black Marines, would end up serving in pioneer or labor units, for the need for logistic support troops in the Pacific fighting was acute.

Colonel Woods visted Headquarters Marine Corps in January and presented a plan for the future development of Montford Point. He indicated the 51st could carry on the handling of all black Marines through February and into March when a new 1,000-man camp area would be ready. Simultaneously, organization work would be underway on the Mess Attendants School (an 8-week course) and an Officers' Cooks and Stewards School (a 16-week course). The contemplated increase in black Marines would dictate the organization of a separate Montford Point Camp headquarters by late spring.[32]

In January, the first 42 selective service men arrived at Montford Point to be treated no differently as boots than the men who had gone before them. Many of the draftees, both then and later, were selective service volunteers. Marine liaison officers with the Selective Service System and Marine recruiters worked mightily to ensure that most of the draftees were men who wanted to serve in the Corps. The experiences of a number of men who entered during this period bear out the continued effort at enlisting the best men available.[33] In May, Colonel Woods wrote the Commandant that "the standard of inductees continues to be about the same as in the case of volunteers. This indicates excellent work by the recruiting service."[34]

Change continued at Montford Point during the first half of 1943. In January, the first black NCOs were appointed as three assistant cooks, Jerome D. Alcorn, Otto Cherry, and Robert T. Davis, were named field cooks (corporals) on the 18th. Men who had been assigned to tactical units of the 51st, but who had demonstrated that they were of DI caliber while in boot camp, rejoined Battery A in February. Ten of them made corporal on the 19th, the nucleus for a vastly increased recruit training effort. Nineteen other new corporals were made in other units of the 51st in February and thereafter new NCOs were appointed every month.

On 11 March, Headquarters and Service Company, Headquarters Battalion, Montford Point Camp was activated, as was Headquarters Company, Recruit Depot Battalion. Battery A of the 51st became Company A of the Recruit Depot Battalion. Colonel Woods, as camp commander, relinquished his command of the 51st to Lieutenant Colonel W. Bayard Onley, a Naval Academy graduate (1919) who had recently served as Executive Officer, 23d Marines,[35] and Lieutenant Colonel Holdahl took over the new recruit battalion. On 1 April 1943, Headquarters Company, Messman Branch Battalion was organized with the new battalion commander Captain Albert O. Madden, a World War I veteran who had been recommissioned as a food service officer after extensive restaurant experience in the Albany, New York, area.[36] The new unit with its attendant schools was redesignated Stewards' Branch Battalion on 13 April. The new camp area which would house the stewards was dubbed "Slotnick's Grove" by the black Marines after a young lieutenant who had been involved in its construction.[37]

Reorganization and augmentation continued at a frantic pace as hundreds of recruits poured into Montford Point. New recruit companies were organized, a Schools Company and a Motor Transport Company were added to the camp headquarters battalion, the 51st's Rifle Company became the vehicle for organizing and dispatching depot companies (labor troops) to the field, and an Assistant Stewards' School (Company A) and a Stewards' Cook School (Company B) were added to Captain Madden's battalion.

The change on the recruit drill field was the most drastic. Almost all of the SES DIs had left by the end of April; black sergeants and corporals took over as the senior DIs of the eight platoons then in training: the 16th Platoon (Edgar R. Huff); 17th (Thomas Brokaw); 18th (Charles E. Allen); 19th (Gilbert H. Johnson); 20th (Arnold R. Bostic); 21st (Mortimer A. Cox); 22d (Edgar R. Davis, Jr.); and 23d (George A. Jackson).[38] In late May, the last white drill instructor, First Sergeant Robert W. Colwell, was transferred, and Sergeant "Hashmark" Johnson took his place as the re-

Corporal Edgar R. Huff, one of the first black drill instructors, confronts a recruit platoon at Montford Point. (USMC Photo 5337).

cruit battalion's field sergeant major, in charge of all drill instructors; Sergeant Thomas Pridgen was his assistant. From then on, all recruit training at Montford Point was conducted by black NCOs–a milestone had been passed.

Boot camp did not get any easier, in fact, in the testimony of those who served there in the transition period it became rougher and stayed rougher.[39] The boots started on the run and stayed on the run. As one black DI commented: "Glenn Cunningham [a famous miler] had nothing on the recruits at Montford Point."[40] "Hashmark" Johnson, first as field sergeant major and later as sergeant major of the Recruit Depot Battalion, was determined that the black boots would measure up in every way to Marine Corps standards. His philosophy prevaded boot training. In later years, addressing a group of veterans of that era, he reminded them of their ordeal and the reason for it, remarking:

> I was an ogre to some of you that met me on the drill field and in the huts of Montford more than a quarter century ago. I was a stern instructor, but I was fair. I was an exacting instructor, but with some understanding of the many problems involved. I kept before me, always, that nearly impossible goal to qualify in a few weeks, and at the most a few months, a type of Marine fully qualified in every respect to wear that much cherished Globe and Anchor. You were untried. The objectives were to qualify you with loyalty, with a devotion to duty, and with a determination equal to all, transcended by none . . . As I look into your faces tonight, I remember the youthful, and sometimes pained expressions at something I may have said . . . But I remember something you did. You measured up, by a slim margin perhaps, but measure up you did. You achieved your goal. That realization creates within me a warm appreciation of you and a deep sense of personal gratitude.[41]

With Johnson's type of drive permeating the boot camp at the man-to-man level of DI and recruit, life proved to be very trying for the new Marines. But it was not all drill and training. There were USO shows and movies at the camp theatre and a full schedule of intramural sports between various units at the camp. And there was always music, for many talented singers and musicians had enlisted. Men from the bands of Count Basie, Cab Calloway, Duke Ellington, and Erskine Hawkins were in the ranks of the 51st's band, which later became the camp band. The band was capable of producing jazz combos, dance orchestras, and concert groups of professional caliber.

Fortunately, one of the young officers who arrived early at Montford Point was Lieutenant Robert W. Troup, Jr., an accomplished composer and musician from New York, who established immediate rapport with the black musicians which carried over to the rest of the men. He eventually became camp recreation officer, and many of his activities were directly connected with the improvement of morale through the arrangement of talent shows, sporting events, and concerts using the multitude of entertainment and athletic talent in the ranks at Montford Point. He elicited almost universal praise for understanding, ranging from "Hashmark" Johnson's typically restrained, "a top-notch musician, a very decent sort of officer," to Obie Hall's, "he was the sharpest cat I ever seen in my life."[42] But most of the men of Montford Point remember Bobby Troup's song "Jacksonville," which hardly rivaled his World War II hit "Route 66" in nationwide popular music charts, but certainly was a hit at Camp Lejeune where it echoed the sentiments of black and white Marines alike with words like:

Take me away from Jacksonville, 'cause I've had my fill and that's no lie,

Take me away from Jacksonville, keep me away from Jacksonville until I die,

Jacksonville stood still while the rest of the world passed by.[43]

Black Marines practice descending cargo nets in Montford Point's training pool under the watchful eye of Sergeant Paul E. Meeres (on board). (USMC Photo 8275).

Near mid-summer, one of the frequent entertainments that featured Montford Point talent, a series of boxing matches plus unarmed combat exhibitions by Tony Ghazlo and his instructors, produced an incident that has never left the memory of any man who witnessed it. Major General Henry L. Larsen, who had just returned from the South Pacific to take command of Camp Lejeune, was invited to attend this "boxing smoker" and took the occasion to make a short speech to the assembled black Marines. There are as many versions of his exact words as there are witnesses, but the gist of his remarks, as remembered, was that when he had come back from overseas he had not realized how serious the war situation was until he had seen "you people wearing our uniform." [44] The unfriendly response from the predominently black audience was immediate and tumultuous. His unfortunate choice of words emphasized to the men that they were still on trial in the eyes of many white Marines.

By early fall, when Bobby Troup's popular farewell to Jacksonville was being sung, whistled, and played throughout Monford Point, many men had already left the North Carolina camp. When the anniversary date of the opening of Montford Point was reached, four depot companies had already deployed overseas, and a Marine barracks detachment had been sent to the Naval Ammunition Depot, McAlester, Oklahoma. The 51st had locked on to a train-

Marines from Montford Point climb down a cargo net into a waiting LCVP for a practice landing at Onslow Beach. (USMC Photo 9007).

ing schedule for overseas deployment, other depot companies were forming for duty in the Pacific, and stewards were leaving for assignment to officers' messes in the states and overseas. The pace of the camp quickened as more and more men left for duty beyond the reaches of Montford Point. The test of combat was yet to come for black Marine units, but it was inevitable.

CHAPTER 2

THE 51ST DEFENSE BATTALION

Throughout the first six months that blacks served in the Marine Corps, the focus of attention was the 51st Composite Defense Battalion. It was to be the first (and for a time, the only) black combat unit. Its initial stages of training were hampered by equipment shortages, but even more by the complete unfamiliarity of the men with the weapons and supporting equipment they encountered. There were a number of qualified white instructors for the various specialties, and many of the junior officers had attended short technical courses of various types, but the biggest drawback to the battalion's progress in training was the fact that it had no cadre of experienced men on which to build.

The initial selection of men the battalion received in its new tactical units was a good one, but many of these served only briefly in its ranks before they moved on to the drill field, to schools, and to camp offices to help cope with the swelling tide of draftees, or to the depot companies that began forming in March and April. As a consequence, there were only about 500 men on the rolls of the 51st on 21 April 1943 when a new commanding officer fresh from overseas, Lieutenant Colonel Floyd A. Stephenson, arrived at Montford Point to take over. His predecessor, Lieutenant Colonel Onley, moved on to take command of the camp Headquarters Battalion and to serve as Colonel Wood's executive officer.

Lieutenant Colonel Stephenson was an experienced artillery officer who had been at Pearl Harbor with the 4th Defense Battalion when the Japanese attacked. Later, he served as the battalion's executive officer and commander of its 5-inch artillery group at Efate in the New Hebrides.[1] He approached his new task with enthusiasm and considerable drive. Within two weeks, he was recommending that the 51st become a regular, heavy defense battalion and stating "that there is nothing that suitable colored personnel can not be taught."[2] Colonel Woods in his favorable en-

dorsement to Stephenson's recommendation indicated that he was "now fully convinced that this unit can be forged into a first class fighting outfit in a reasonably short time after its complement is filled." He also noted that a composite defense battalion was designed "to meet the requirements of a situation that no longer exists."[3]

The units that would be detached from the 51st, if the change took place, would be the Rifle Company (Reinforced) and the 75mm Pack Howitzer Battery. A Machine Gun Group had been organized on 1 March 1943 to give the battalion a light antiaircraft capability and it would remain together with the 155mm and 90mm guns.

The recommendation was approved at Headquarters Marine Corps on 28 May 1943

90mm antiaircraft gun crew of the 51st Defense Battalion practices loading shells at Montford Point. (USMC Photo 9507).

with the stipulation that men under training for infantry and field artillery would continue to train with the 51st pending organization of a separate infantry battalion.[4] The news of the change caused some bewilderment and consternation among the black Marines at Montford Point. The inclusion of infantry and field artillery in the 51st had meant to most men that the battalion would see some close combat. The purpose of separating and redesignating these units was widely misunderstood. Reinforcing this misunderstanding was the loss, earlier in the year, of the light tank platoon which had been part of the rifle company. Although some defense battalions already overseas had such platoons, they were no longer to be an integral part of the defense battalion organization. Rumor had it that the black Marines would serve only as labor troops or officers' stewards.

The First Combat Unit

Fortunately, the rumor was soon dispelled insofar as the 51st was concerned. On 7 June 1943, "Composite" was dropped from the title of the 51st Defense Battalion. The 155mm Gun Battery expanded to become the 155mm Artillery Group and the Machine Gun Group became the Special Weapons Group, its principal armament now being 20mm and 40mm cannon as well as .50 caliber machine guns. Rifle Company (Reinforced) was redesignated Company A, 7th Separate Infantry Battalion and the 75s became the 7th Separate Pack Howitzer Battery. Both units were attached to the camp's Headquarters Battalion but were stationed in the 51st's area to continue training with the defense battalion.

The redesignations continued in July when the 155s became the Seacoast Artillery Group and the 90s the Antiaircraft Artillery Group, in keeping with the titles of such units in a new table of organization for defense battalions.[5] The summer was fully occupied with intensive training on weapons, fire control equipment, searchlights, and all the myriad of equipment that a defense battalion possessed. A few men were sent away to specialist schools at various Army bases and some received schooling at Camp Lejeune, but the vast majority learned on the job. The battalion doubled in size in July, and the growth continued in succeeding months, with over 1,700 officers and men on

the rolls in October. Not all these Marines were destined to serve in the 51st, however.

Lieutenant Colonel Stephenson had been given the task of assimilating and training the cadre of another defense battalion, approximately 400 men, at the same time he readied his own troops for combat. The new unit, the 52d Defense Battalion, was to be organized at the start of 1944.[6]

The increased pace of training was marred by the death on 20 August of the first black to die in Marine Corps uniform, Corporal Gilbert Fraser, Jr. of the 51st's Seacoast Artillery Group. Fraser, a New Yorker who had attended Virginia Union College, was killed when he fell 30 feet from a landing net into a landing boat while his unit was practicing debarkation. A road leading from the main camp at Montford Point to the base artillery area was named after the popular 30-year-old Marine. Lieutenant Colonel Stephenson noted Fraser Road would be "a constant reminder to those who come after him of the fine type of young manhood" represented by Gilbert Fraser.[7]

In early September, the battalion moved out of Montford Point proper across Scales Creek to the old CCC-Camp Knox area where it took over three of four barracks blocks; the other was occupied by the War Dog Training Center. The accomodations in the new campsite were not luxurious; the barracks, mess halls, and offices were old wooden buildings, drafty and badly in need of repair.[8] The living quarters were characterized by one of the 51st as "more open than closed" and dominated by big pot-bellied stoves. He recalled that if you stood within 10 feet of them "you roasted in front and froze behind."[9] But the move was popular with the battalion. It was off by itself, running its own show, and the transfer across Scales Creek intensified the feeling of the men of the 51st that they were a bit different, superior even, to the rest of the blacks at Montford Point. In the battalion's news column in the Camp Lejeune paper, the writer, Sergeant Jimmie Stewart, observed: "We just can't get over the thrill of being here at Camp Knox. Boy, its really swell. Makes us feel like we're in the groove again and that life is not so bad after all."[10]

Most of the reason the men of the 51st "thought they were the cat's meow," as one member put it, was that they were in the only black Marine unit engaged in extensive combat training.[11] They considered themselves to be members of a fighting outfit and were not at all hesitant about reminding the other black Marines of the fact. On liberty they stuck together, a not unusual trait of men from units with high morale. They were convinced, and not without some reason, that most of the men at Montford Point wanted to serve in the 51st.

The battalion's lot throughout the fall of 1943 was hard, exhausting training. First the Seacoast Group moved out to Onslow Beach to fire its 155s; the Antiaircraft and Special Weapons Groups soon followed to test their gunnery. The whole battalion spent two months in the field, a period that saw hard usage for all its equipment in frequently miserable weather. In order to fill the ranks of the augmented 51st, many men with no recruit training and others with only a few days of boot camp were added to the firing batteries so that they could get target practice experience, and the battalion would be ready to mount out at full strength on schedule.[12] It made the task of the officers and white instructor NCOs doubly difficult to have to supervise these raw recruits and train the "veterans," who were not long out of boot camp themselves. Still, the job

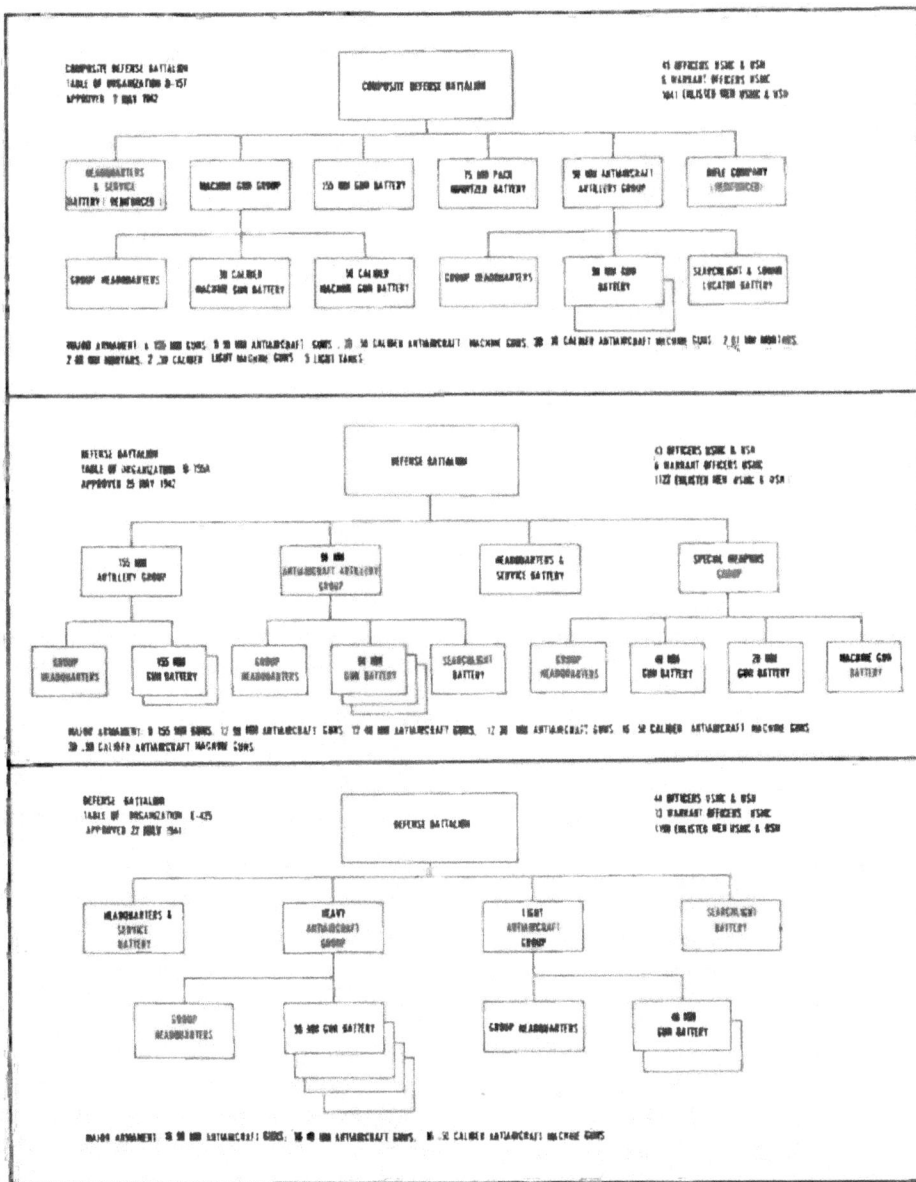

DEFENSE BATTALIONS 1942-1946

was done, although a number of the officers noted in their December training reports and in later comments that they thought the 51st needed more training before going overseas, that the newly promoted black NCOs needed more seasoning, and that in general the men, most of whom had had no experience with sophisticated equipment, "showed a lack of appreciation of the value or importance of material and equipment." [13]

These judgments did not obviate the fact that men had often done quite well at target practice at Onslow Beach. When an inspecting party including Secretary Knox and General Holcomb watched the 90mm guns being fired in November, the gun crews shot down the towed target within 60 seconds after they started firing. Lieutenant Colonel Stephenson reported General Holcomb as remarking, "I think they're ready now." [14] And "What a yelp went up" amongst the black Marines when they hit that target: to them it proved too that they were ready. [15]

Not long after the battalion returned to Camp Knox in early December, Lieutenant Colonel Stephenson went to Headquarters Marine Corps to get further orders on the future of the 51st. Much to his dismay he found that the battalion's sailing orders had been moved up five weeks from original plans and that the 52d Defense Battalion was also to be organized two weeks ahead of the original projection. Plans for sending the men who had joined as recruits to the rifle range to complete that essential part of their training had to be scrapped and holiday leaves cancelled. The 400-odd men destined for the 52d were transferred out of the 51st and the new battalion was formed on 15 December. Plans for special training of the seacoast artillery in field artillery firing techniques were put aside and all officers and men away at school were recalled. All hands turned to at a furious pace to crate and pack the battalion's equipment for the pending move. [16]

Another sure sight that the battalion was on its way was the transfer of the white senior NCOs and instructors to other units at Camp Lejeune. The blacks who had been their assistants now took over. Gunnery Sergeant Charles W. Simmons became the battalion sergeant major. He later recalled: "I will never forget the consternation of the white sergeant who trained me for the job of Sergeant Major of the 51st, when we learned that he would not

go overseas with the battalion. I was surprised too—but I understand the situation. I had graduated!" [17]

In early January, 175 freight cars were loaded at the rate of 25 a day, mostly in rotten weather with heavy doses of rain, snow, and sleet. [18] The men turned to with a will, however, since they were sure they were headed for combat. The battalion moved out in increments with the seacoast artillery leading off and the rest of the units followed in their own troop trains. By 19 January, only a relatively small rear echelon was left at Camp Knox, and it too was slated to leave the next day.

The departure of the 51st was not without incident that became a matter of controversy and investigation. What started out to be some farewell rounds of beer by rear echelon members at the Montford Point snack bar deteriorated into a conflict with the military police. When the confrontation reached the bottle-throwing stage, the MP sergeant on the scene closed the snack bar. As some of the 51st's men started to throw rocks at him, he fired his carbine in the air three times in warning, and the crowd dispersed.

Later that evening, about 15 or 20 shots were fired from the Camp Knox area towards Montford Point. Unfortunately, one of these random shots, which were judged to be firings with no intent to hit anyone, did find a target. Corporal Rolland J. Curtiss, a drill instructor who had his platoon in the woods back of the camp theatre, was wounded, though not seriously.

Authorities soon made checks of all the rifles in the Camp Knox area but could not determine conclusively if any had been fired. There was evidence, however, of some laxity in the accountability of rifles in the battalion. This became a feature of a critical report that Colonel Woods submitted to the Commandant after the departure of the last elements of the 51st for the west coast. He commented unfavorably on the police of certain parts of the camp, that numerous items of personal equipment had been left behind, and that the care of government property had been neglected. [19]

So it happened that the 51st Defense Battalion arrived at San Diego under somewhat of a cloud. Most of the men in the battalion were unaware of the events that had transpired. They were proudly wearing their new battalion shoulder patch, issued just before they left

Religious services are held at Onslow Beach for men of the 51st's Seacoast Artillery Group. In the background is one of the group's 155mm guns. (Photo from Montford Point Pictorial).

Camp Lejeune.[20] It was a red oval with a large white "51" in the center with the white letters "USMC" below and a blue 90mm antiaircraft gun superimposed on the numerals. As they moved into tents at Camp Elliott, some of the men went to the base's open air movie and disrupted the show when they were told blacks had to sit in the back of the amphitheatre. They were not having any part of segregation that night; they were too full of themselves as combat-bound Marines. Despite the fracas, Lieutenant Colonel Stephenson authorized the issuance of liberty passes.[21]

On 27 January 1944, much to the disappointment of the men, who liked and respected Stephenson, the battalion was assigned a new commanding officer, and Stephenson was transferred. Colonel Curtis W. LeGette, the new commander, was a veteran artillery officer who had originally entered the Marine Corps as an enlisted man in 1910. He had just returned to the states from a tour of duty as commanding officer of the 7th Defense Battalion in the Ellice Islands.[22] Soon after he took over, he fell the battalion in and gave the men a dressing down on the subject of their discipline and general behavior. Naturally enough, he used the term "you people," a common expression in the Marine Corps by a superior when addressing a group of men, but to the men of the 51st it meant "you blacks" and the lecture fell on deaf ears.[23]

Overseas Duty

Much to the young blacks surprise, all of the weapons and equipment that they had packed so laboriously on the east coast were now turned in to the quartermasters at Camp Elliott and San Diego. The men retained only their personal gear and the battalion only a modest amount of its property. On 11 February, the 51st boarded a merchant transport, SS *Meteor*, at San Diego and sailed. The ship's destination was the Ellice Islands, where the 51st was destined to relieve the 7th Defense Battalion. En route to the islands, on 23 February, Detachment A, 51st Defense Battalion was organized with approximately half the men in the battalion on its rolls and Lieutenant Colonel Gould P. Groves, the battalion executive officer, as its commander. The mission of the new detachment was to provide a garrison for Nanomea Island. The rest of the battalion under Colonel LeGette was headed for Funafuti and would outpost Nukufetau.

Moving by landing ship and submarine chaser, Detachment A reached Nanomea on 25 February 1944; the rest of the battalion disembarked at Funafuti on the 27th.[24] In both places the men of the 51st found the Marines of the 7th Defense Battalion eager to leave. "They were never so glad to see black people in their lives," one of the new arrivals at Nanomea decided.[25] The 51st took over the equipment and weapons of the 7th Defense, much of which had seen hard usage since the battalion had first reached the South Pacific nine months before Pearl Harbor was attacked.

The task assigned the detachment on Nanomea and the outpost on Nukefetau was to maintain and defend the airfields on those islands for emergency use. On Funafuti, Colonel LeGette was charged with maintaining existing staging and limited repair facilities for aircraft, an anchorage and a motor torpedo boat base, and with defending the atoll. The airfields in the Ellice Islands were on standby to support combat operations then going on in the Marshall Islands to the northward.

Not much exciting happened to the 51st in its first overseas assignment, although the 155mm gun crews on Nanomea did let loose 11 rounds at a suspected enemy submarine on 28 March. Most of the time was spent on gun drill and firing practice, and the battalion began to shake down into a settled outfit, though it still did not entirely please its more senior officers, many of whom were veterans of oversea service with other defense battalions in the early part of the war.

In June, when a letter from the Commandant arrived at Funafuti indicating that the 51st's ordnance and motor transport equipment left behind in California showed signs of lack of proper preventive maintenance, Col-

40mm gun crew of the 51st Defense Battalion ready to fire target practice at Montford Point. (Photo from Montford Point Pictorial).

onel LeGette ordered a board of investigation and appointed himself the examining officer.[26] The lengthy study, which included testimony from battery and group commanders, arrived at a conclusion that the former commanding officer of the battalion was primarily at fault.[27] When Colonel LeGette followed up this investigation report with an unfavorable report the next month on the state of the 51st's combat efficiency, Lieutenant Colonel Stephenson was embarked on a long siege of letter writing to Washington to tell his side of the story. Much of the correspondence forms the basis for what is known about the state of the 51st's training and capabilities, at least from the standpoint of the battalion's officers. Throughout his embattled responses, Stephenson, who was overseas with the 6th Marine Division at the time, maintained a strong defense of his actions and of the unit he had trained, calling it "the finest organization in the whole Negro program in the Marine Corps. . . ."[28] It should be noted that much of this exchange went on without the knowledge of the men in the ranks of the 51st Defense Battalion. In their own eyes, they had done well and were steadily improving their capabilities.

Another of the frequent changes in the battalion's organization occurred in July. As a result of a Marine Corps-wide reshuffling of tables of organization for defense battalions, most units were redesignated as antiaircraft artillery battalions. Their seacoast artillery groups were disbanded or reorganized into field artillery battalions of the corps artillery of the two Marine amphibious corps in the Pacific. The 51st Defense Battalion, the 52d, and the 6th on Midway were the only units to retain their original titles, although the primary function of all three battalions was now antiaircraft defense.[29] On 15 July 1944, the Seacoast Artillery Group of the 51st was disbanded and its men transferred to other units of the battalion. The 90s became a Heavy Antiaircraft Group, Special Weapons became a Light Antiaircraft Group, and a separate Searchlight Battery was organized.

At about the same time these changes were occurring, the 51st's detachments on Nanomea and Nukufetau began moving to Funafuti. Detachment A was disbanded on 15 July, and the battalion began preparations to move to a more forward area. While these activities were going on, the Commandant, Samoan Defense Group, Captain Allen Hobbs, USN, who was

LeGette's senior, wrote the colonel to express "his appreciation for the excellent spirit and efficient manner in which the officers and men of this battalion have carried out their duties under trying and difficult conditions." He further wished the 51st "luck and profitable hunting in your new assignment." [30]

On to the Marshalls

Once again the weapons and equipment of the 51st had been using were packed and turned in. In the opinion of one member of the motor transport section, which had had to rebuild many of vehicles it had inherited from the 7th Defense Battalion, "everything was standing tall when we left." [31] The unit went on board ship, the Dutch-manned U.S. Army transport *Kota Agoeng,*[32] early in September, sailing on the 8th. The new destination was Eniwetok Atoll, a bustling support area for the operations just concluded in the Mariana Islands.

On 14 September, the battalion arrived at Eniwetok and in the next three days replaced elements of the 10th Antiaircraft Battalion, taking over its weapons and equipment on Eniwetok, Engebi, Parry, and Porky Islands. The 10th was formally relieved on 17 September and left for Pearl Harbor on the *Kota Agoeng.*[33] The 51st, almost as soon as it was settled in position, embarked on an intensive schedule of training and towed-sleeve firing. The radar and searchlight units were constantly busy as aircraft based on the atoll were used to try to penetrate the battalion's defensive screen. There were Japanese on bypassed islands in the Marshalls, and the men were readily aware that they were a lot closer to the shooting war. The enormous lagoon at Eniwetok was a constantly shifting scene as ships passed through going and coming from the forward areas. Here, at least, there was the possibility of action and spirits perked up.

The men of the 51st really sharpened their talents as gunners at Eniwetok. The battalion became a veteran unit; towed-sleeve targets were shot down with regularity, searchlights pinpointed their targets as soon as they "struck arc," and the radar operators prided themselves in detecting any and all snoopers.[34] But the fact of the matter remained that the first black Marine combat unit was not in combat.

On 13 December 1944, Colonel LeGette relinquished command of the 51st to return to the States. When he left he expressed regret that he could not stay with the battalion throughout its overseas tour.[35] The new and last commander of the 51st was its former executive officer, Lieutenant Colonel Groves, who had joined it at Montford Point in 1943.

There was action for the battalion at Eniwetok, but nothing of substance. In early February there was a week-long submarine alert with many contacts but no sightings. Later in the spring, Condition Red was sounded, and the men raced gleefully and hopefully to their positions, but no enemy planes appeared. Their disappointment was bitter. No matter how well trained the battalion became, there was bound to be a letdown in morale. One former sergeant recalled, "the routine got so boresome, but we got a few plane crashes, a couple once in a while; a ship would go down at sea trying to land, but other than that they were disappointed they didn't actually get into combat. That was what they really wanted." [36]

On 12 June 1945, a detachment of one 90mm gun battery, one 40mm platoon, and four searchlight sections was formed at Eniwetok for duty at Kwajalein Atoll. Christened Composite Group, 51st Defense Battalion under Major William M. Tracy, the 251-man unit left Eniwetok by LST on the 14th and disembarked at Kwajalein on 17 June; the rear echelon arrived on the 22d. There the group's duties were the same of those of the remainder of the battalion, antiaircraft defense of an atoll. And like the rest of the 51st, the Composite Group saw no combat action in the war.

Home Again

Once the fighting was over, the Marines in the 51st Defense Battalion were itching to get home. Since the unit had been overseas for 19 months when the war ended and had received no replacements, many of the men were close to the point discharge total projected for the end of the year. The 51st was ripe for return to the States as a unit. The men had started out together, gone through the war together, and now they would go home together.

On 20 November at Kwajalein and 21 November at Eniwetok, detachments of the 52d Defense Battalion arrived from Guam to replace the 51st. The reunion of the two black units was fleeting for the men returning home immediately boarded the ships that had brought the 52d. On 21 November, the Com-

A veteran 90mm crew of the 51st Defense Battalion poses with its gun. "Lena Horne," at Eniwetok in 1945. (USMC Photo 121743).

posite Group sailed on the attack cargo ship USS *Wyandot* (AKA—92) for Pearl Harbor, where the ship stayed a few days before it steamed on for the Panama Canal and the east coast. On Thanksgiving Day, 22 November, the main body of the 51st left Eniwetok without regret and headed for San Diego on another cargo ship, the USS *Sibik* (AK—121). Save for the rough thumping that catching the tail end of a severe storm in an empty ship can give you, the trip back was uneventful.

On 10 December, the *Sibik* docked at San Diego, and the battalion moved to Camp Pendleton, where those men who lived west of the Mississippi and had enough points were discharged. The majority entrained on the 19th and reached Camp Lejeune on Christmas Day 1945, where the men from the Composite Group rejoined. They had returned to Montford Point by way of Norfolk on 21 December.

The processing of the high point men for discharge began almost immediately. The of-

ficers who had long served with the battalion began leaving. After Lieutenant Colonel Groves departed on 7 January, the acting commanding officer for the rest of the month was a second lieutenant. But there was not much of an outfit left for him to command as the discharges continued. On 31 January 1946, the 51st Defense Battalion was formally disbanded and the remaining low point men were transferred to other units at Montford Point.

As the men went their separate ways, they took with them the knowledge that they had served in a unique, a pioneering unit, and had shared its ups and downs. Possessed of an almost cocky belief in themselves as Marines and a special pride in their battalion besides, they had not needed combat to develop self respect. As a black correspondent who visited the 51st at Eniwetok in October 1945 noted about its men: "They are a grand bunch! And because of their ability to come through the kind of experience they have had, with its attendant racial irritants, they undoubtedly will be better men and better citizens." [37]

CHAPTER 3

THE 52D DEFENSE BATTALION

Many of the troubles that had plagued the 51st Defense Battalion in its infancy were greatly lessened for the 52d. The key to its relatively smooth training period was the cadre of 400 officers and men that had spent three to six months in the 51st. They brought their experience on the antiaircraft and seacoast defense guns, searchlights, height and range finders, and other technical equipment with them. They were soon joined in the early part of 1944 by the experienced field artillerymen of the 7th Separate Pack Howitzer Battery, which was disbanded on 31 March. The cadre and the pack howitzer men made up more than a third of the strength of the new battalion. The 52d was in far better shape than the 51st had been to rely on on-the-job training, using experienced blacks to train others.

The new battalion's commanding officer, a native Floridian, Colonel Augustus W. Cockrell, had spent a year at West Point and then four years as a Marine enlisted man before he was commissioned in 1922. Cockrell, like many of his field officers and battery commanders, was already a veteran of overseas service in World War II. He had been executive officer of the 2d Defense Battalion in Samoa when the war broke out and had commanded the 8th Defense Battalion in Samoa and on Wallis Island until August 1943.[1] Known respectfully as "old Gus" to the black NCOs who served most closely with him, Colonel Cockrell was a good choice to oversee the formative months of the battalion.

In addition to the fact that one out of three men in the 52d was a Marine with some antiaircraft, seacoast, or field artillery experience, there was also another aspect of the battalion which pleased its officers. The senior black NCOs had some time under their belts, certainly not as much as white NCOs of comparable rank, but for the most part they had been around Montford Point for a year or more. Just as important, they were not trying to command men they had gone through boot camp with. They had had some seasoning as military leaders and were more aware of the responsibilities of their rank.

Not only did Colonel Cockrell have a more favorable ratio of experienced NCOs and men in the 52d than Lieutenant Colonel Stephenson had had in the 51st, he also managed to increase the number of men who received technical school training in their respective specialties. When the 52d moved into the 51st's old quarters at Camp Knox in February and began training in earnest, its prospects for effective end results were far better than those of the 51st had been. The morale in the new outfit was excellent, helped on as the 51st's had been by a distinctive battalion shoulder patch that set the men apart from the other units at Montford Point. The 52d's colorful insignia featured a red shield with a blue diagonal bar across the center supporting four white stars; in the upper left corner was a gold shell burst with a scarlet "52" on it and in the lower right was a gold 90mm gun and mount with a scarlet "USMC" superimposed.

Following the pattern of the 51st, the 52d also took to the sand dunes and scrub growth of Onslow Beach for firing practice as its training program progressed. And like defense battalions throughout the Marine Corps it lost its seacoast artillery group on 12 June 1944 in the universal reorganization of these units to antiaircraft artillery battalions. Most of the 292 officers and men who had manned the 155mm guns were transferred to the heavy antiaircraft group, where an additional 90mm battery was formed. The light antiaircraft group dropped its 20mm guns and added another 40mm battery, and a new searchlight battery was formed.

Shortly after this reorganization, the battalion also lost its first commanding officer as Colonel Cockrell was transferred to camp headquarters where he was slated to replace Colonel Woods. On 12 July 1944 Lieutenant

Colonel Joseph W. Earnshaw took command of the battalion. A native of Kansas and graduate of the Naval Academy (Class of 1927), he had come to Montford Point from Washington where he had spent two years in the Planning Division of the Navy's Bureau of Ordnance. At the outbreak of the war, he had served as technical advisor to the Army's commander in the Society Islands. Like his predecessor, Lieutenant Colonel Earnshaw was an experienced artillery officer.[2]

August 1944 saw the battalion end its training at Montford Point. Its weapons and equipment were cleaned, checked, and turned in to the quartermaster at Camp Lejeune. Like the 51st, it would make its move overseas traveling light. As a necessary preliminary to that move the battalion was completely reorganized on 15 August. In effect two nearly identical half battalions were formed, each containing a headquarters and service group and a heavy antiaircraft group with an equal proportion of gun, searchlight, and equipment crews and other specialists. Lieutenant Colonel Thomas C. Moore, Jr., the battalion executive officer, took command of Detachment A, 52d Defense Battalion. Moore, from Georgia and a graduate of Georgia Tech, had served overseas with the 3d Defense Battalion in the Guadalcanal campaign. He had joined the 52d in May 1944 after serving for some time with the Artillery Battalion of the Training Center at Camp Lejeune.[3]

On 19 August, the two new administrative units of the battalion entrained together at Camp Lejeune and headed west.

First to the Marshalls

After an uneventful cross-country trip, the 52d arrived at Camp Pendleton on 24 August. Nearly a month was spent encamped in the barren hills of Pendleton, but it was a month that included some liberty in the coastal towns and cities. Some of the men from other parts of the country learned to like the Golden State so much during their brief stay there that they asked to be discharged in California when they later returned from overseas.[4]

On 21 September 1944, both administrative units of the battalion boarded the transport USS *Winged Arrow* (AP–170) at San Diego, sailing the same day for Pearl Harbor. Six days later, the ship arrived at Oahu and then lay berthed in the Navy Yard for a week and a half

75mm pack howitzer gun crew trains on the piece at Montford Point. (Photo from Montford Point Pictorial).

with the troops on board. The *Winged Arrow* got underway on 8 October, this time headed south for the Marshall Islands. Majuro Atoll was its first destination.

Majuro, which was situated on the eastern edge of the Marshalls, was the home base for the scout bomber squadrons of Marine Aircraft Group (MAG) 13 and of the 1st Antiaircraft Artillery (AAA) Battalion which protected its airstrips. Detachment A disembarked at Majuro on 17 October to relieve the 1st AAA Battalion which had been part of the original landing force when the atoll was occupied in February 1944.[5]

The remainder of the 52d Defense Battalion sailed on to the westward, to Kwajalein Atoll in the center of the Marshalls. Arriving at the twin islands of Roi-Namur on the 18th, the battalion stayed on board ship for several days before landing on the 22d. It relieved the 15th AAA Battalion of its mission of guarding the airfield and installations that housed the fighter squadrons of MAG–31. Like Detachment A at Majuro, the half of the 52d at Roi-Namur was soon hard at work test firing the guns it had taken over, holding tracking drills, and in general getting settled into position.

The prime mission of the Marine aircraft at Majuro and Roi-Namur was to continue the neutralization of the Japanese garrisons that existed on Wotje, Maloelap, Mille, and Jaluit Atolls. Although no known aircraft still existed at these Japanese bases, the enemy did possess the ability to repair the airfields there and planes might be flown in for supply, evacuation, or reconnaissance purposes.[6] Although the possibility of a Japanese air attack was remote, it existed, and this was the reason for the 52d's presence, with one antiaircraft battalion replacing two as a reduced scale of air defense was called for.

Lieutenant Colonel Moore's detachment at Majuro, in addition to its air defense duties, found itself acting as reconnaissance Marines. Monthly after the detachment arrived, patrols of 60–65 men from the firing batteries would board naval landing craft and check out the atolls, mostly Erikub and Aur, which lay between Majuro and the nearest Japanese bases. These two-to-six day excursions were generally uneventful, although a Battery C patrol to Tabal Island in December brought in three Japanese prisoners the natives had taken, and a Battery D patrol to Aur in January brought back 186 natives to be resettled at Kwajalein.

The battalion's stay in the Marshalls was only six months long as the war was moving forward to the Western Pacific and the 52d, like many of the Marine units in the islands, was to move with it. MAG–31 was among the units marked for participation in the Okinawa operation, scheduled for 1 April 1945. Rumors were rife amongst the men of the 52d on Roi-Namur that the black battalion would be moving forward with them. Relations between the two units were cordial, even to the extent of the staff NCOs of both setting up an integrated staff club.[7] But the hoped-for joint move was not to be, and MAG–31's ground echelon and its planes departed in March.

The naval activity attending the departure seemed to have attracted enemy submarines, and there was a flurry of action as the 52d's men outposted nearby islands, patrolled others farther away, and manned their guns, but found no targets. Under a new commanding officer, Lieutenant Colonel David W. Silvey, who had relieved Lieutenant Colonel Earnshaw on 10 January, the battalion loaded out on 28 April, boarding a merchantman, the SS *George W. Julian*. Silvey had joined the battalion at Montford Point in May 1944 after

serving with the 6th Defense Battalion at Midway since 1941[8] Since Silvey was junior to Lieutenant Colonel Moore, when the battalion reunited he was destined to become the executive officer while Moore took over the 52d.

The reunion was not too far in the future, for Detachment A had made a move also about a month and a half earlier than the elements at Roi-Namur. On 9 March 1945, the detachment had boarded the transport USS *DeGrasse* (AP–164) at Majuro, taking with it the commendation of the atoll's commander, Captain Harold B. Grow, USNR, who noted to Lieutenant Colonel Moore:

> Your officers have been most cooperative and your men have been examples of deportment, willingness to work, and military behavior. They have been of inestimable value to us in our various armed reconnaissance, and we shall greatly feel your absence.[9]

The destination of both elements of the 52d Defense Battalion was Guam, and the prospect was not bad for further forward movement to combat.

Forward to Guam

Detachment A landed on Guam on 24 March and went ashore to set up camp near Barrigada village on the eastern side of the island just above its narrow waist. It was not long before regular patrols and ambushes were being sent out, for there were hundreds of armed Japanese troops still loose in the jungles on the island, men who had gone into hiding when the island was seized in July and August 1944. Impotent as a combat force, and not very aggressive unless cornered, these stragglers were mainly interested in foraging and staying alive.

Small 10-man patrols and ambush groups were sent out all around the camp area; the use of larger forces was restricted by the dense vegetation which one later patrol commander described as "thick as the hair on a dog's back."[10] The patrols made their first contact on 1 April, killing one of two Japanese discovered within 1,000 yards of the camp. Further sightings were made in the following days, with one of the enemy killed and one wounded on 13 April, another killed on the 21st, and three wounded on the 26th, when an ambush party received return fire, which wounded one member of the 52d, PFC Ernest J. Calland.[11]

Lieutenant Colonel Silvey's group arrived at Guam on 4 May, landed and rejoined the bat-

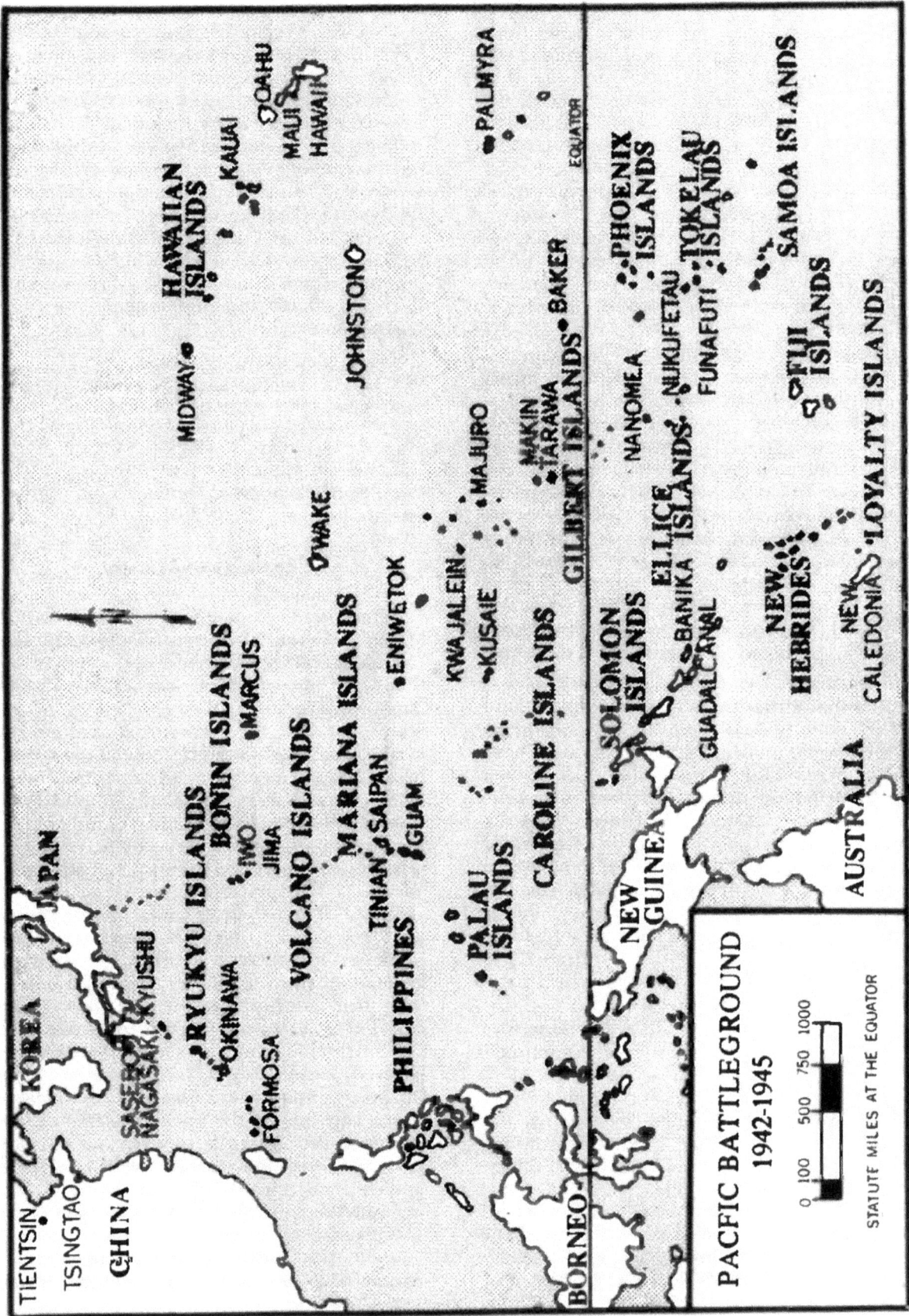

PACFIC BATTLEGROUND
1942-1945

0   100   500   750   1000

STATUTE MILES AT THE EQUATOR

talion. The next day, the 52d, which came under control of the 2d Provisional AAA Group, was directed to undertake intensive training to be accomplished preparatory to movement forward. On 10 May, the formal reorganization of the battalion to its original table of organization took place, and Lieutenant Colonel Moore took command.

As soon as the rest of the 52d was settled in, the intensified round of training and checking equipment began with a readiness date for movement of 15 June. The patrolling and ambushes continued and it was soon obvious that some men had a natural aptitude for the job. Sergeant (later Platoon Sergeant) Ezra Kelly from Mississippi, a member of the Searchlight Battery, was one of these: he killed the first Japanese accounted for by the battalion on Guam and accounted for five others in later patrols.[12] He was, as one of his seniors remarked, "really gung ho. Absolutely fearless." [13]

Insofar as the battalion commander knew, the next destination of the 52d was Okinawa. Loading out for the Ryukyus actually started on 9 July, but the orders were countermanded, and the 52d was directed to remain on Guam, replacing the 9th AAA Battalion. The actual relief of the 9th began on 24 July when Battery C moved into tactical positions with its 90mm guns.

The cancellation of the orders to move forward was unpopular in the 52d. One of the battalion's clerks, PFC John R. Griffith, recalled, "our morale dropped 99%, for the next week or ten days the men stayed around their tents writing letters and what not—mad at the world and everyone in it. Instead of being a Defense Unit, we turned out to be nothing more than a working battalion."[14]

Events had taken a turn for the worse soon after debarkation. On 12 July, the battalion began furnishing Island Command with working parties which grew in strength until by the end of the month nearly half the battalion was working each day, mostly as stevedores. The assignment, much disliked in the 52d, must have amused the men in the black Marine depot companies on Guam, who were heavily committed to this physically demanding work. About this time, Sergeant Major "Hashmark" Johnson appeared from Montford Point and noted with displeasure that "when I arrived the 52d Defense Battalion was performing the duties of a depot company at Apra Harbor." [15]

The new battalion sergeant major was instrumental in getting the patrols and ambushes started again, in fact, the first one that he led himself drew and returned Japanese fire.

The end of the war also saw the end of the tactical employment of the 52d as an antiaircraft battalion. Battery C stood down on 19 August 1945 and after that no unit was tactically emplaced. Concurrent with the move of the battalion to a new camp area formerly occupied by an Army engineer battalion, the 52d began to furnish the 2d Military Police Battalion and Island Command with large daily details of men for guard duty. On 30 September operational control of the defense battalion was passed to the 5th Service Depot, parent command also of the black ammunition and depot companies on the island. Six days later, the battalion began turning in all of its equipment to the depot.

Lieutenant Colonel Moore received word on 18 October that elements of his battalion would be relieving the 51st Defense Battalion at Eniwetok and Kwajalein, so that the older unit could return to the States. In November the battalion split into three parts: Headquarters and Service Battery and the Light Antiaircraft Group stayed on Guam; a composite group designated Battery A (Reinforced), composed of Battery A and four searchlight sections, was told off as the relief at Kwajalein; and the Heavy Antiaircraft Group, less two firing batteries, plus the Searchlight Battery, was set as the relief on Eniwetok. Attached to both the relieving detachments were small groups of high point men who would continue on to the United States with the 51st for discharge.

Both elements of the 52d sailed on 16 November from Guam, on the cargo ships USS *Sibik* (AK-121) for Eniwetok and USS *Wyandot* (AKA-92) for Kwajalein. After the relief of the 51st was effected, the duties of the men at both atolls were non-tactical; there were guard details and general duty chores connected with the winding down of the war effort but little to relieve the boredom. No one was unhappy when word came to return to Guam, since it meant for most men a further return to home.

Postwar Activities

On 29 January 1946, the attack transport USS *Hyde* (APA-173), having picked up the members of the 52d Defense Battalion in the Marshalls, berthed at Guam. A month of change and reorganization followed until on 28 February one of the postwar Pacific units of the Marine Corps destined to be manned by black Marines was formed. Heavy Antiaircraft Group (Provisional), Saipan was activated by redesignation of the 52d's similar group. Low point men were transferred into the new unit, and it began moving piecemeal to Saipan.

Before this happened, however, the ranks of the battalion were thinned even further by the departure of another large group of high point men for the States on 1 February. Among this group were a number of the original Montford Point volunteers of 1942. When their ship arrived in San Francisco on the 22d, they received a pleasant surprise. The receiving barracks were not segregated, nor were those at Camp Pendleton when the men arrived there for processing for discharge.

One gunnery sergeant from Louisiana, Alex "Buck" Johnson, even found himself bossing all-white police details, which he regarded as a welcome change from his previous experience. He noted that contrary to time-honored practice in most units, he did not have to spend his time "running and ducking and looking and trying to find out what happened to my detail." Instead, the men did their work and asked him if there was anything else that he wanted them to do.[16] The imminence of discharge must have disordered the normal proclivity of enlisted Marines to avoid police duties.

The experience of the remainder of the 52d Defense Battalion was more in keeping with the segregated nature of life in the Marine Corps in World War II, since it returned home as a unit. On 13 March 1946, the 357 officers and men still on the rolls of the battalion embarked on the transport USS Wakefield (AP-21) at Guam and sailed for San Diego. Arriving on the 26th, the 52d immediately moved to Camp Pendleton, dropped off the men who had enlisted west of the Mississippi who would be discharged there, and entrained for Camp Lejeune.

On 4 April 1946, the 52d Defense Battalion arrived back at Montford Point Camp. Further discharges and separations took place immediately, and on 21 April Lieutenant Colonel Moore relinquished command of the battalion

he had served with for 23 months. On 15 May 1946, the 52d Defense Battalion passed out of history, redesignated as a new postwar unit to be based at Montford Point, the 3d Antiaircraft Artillery Battalion (Composite).

Neither of the two antiaircraft units that had grown out of the 52d had a long life. The group on Saipan lasted until 28 February 1947 when it was disbanded and its remaining men transferred into provisional depot companies which returned to Guam.[17] The 3d Antiaircraft had a life of 12 months before it too was disbanded on 15 May 1947, with most of its men joining Headquarters Company, Montford Point Camp.[18]

Although not directly responsible for the demise of all black antiaircraft units, the sentiments expressed by Lieutenant Colonel Moore after he had been with the 52d for 20 months are indicative of the line of reasoning that eventually prevailed when the Marine Corps drastically reduced its troop strength in postwar years. He reported to the Commandant that "so long as social conditions make segregation desirable it is believed that Negro Marines could be more advantagously employed in almost any other type unit." He reasoned that antiaircraft units were among the most highly technical in the Marine Corps and needed to draw on the whole Corps for their men, men who would have all possible schools readily available to them as they were not to black Marines. He pointed out that the normal scattered deployment of batteries, radars, and searchlights "defeats the purpose of segregation," because these small units were forced to rely on neighboring organizations for support which would be difficult to get and might not be forthcoming "so long as any evidence of individual racial prejudice continues to exist."[19]

An objective examination of the experiences of the men of the 52d Defense Battalion, weighing all pros and cons, must conclude that despite racial adversity they performed well collectively as Marines. The conclusion is inescapable when one meets veterans of the 52d that both they and the Marine Corps benefited from their service.

CHAPTER 4

DEPOT AND AMMUNITION COMPANIES

One of the ironies of the service of black Marines in World War II was that the units which had been designated, trained, and publicized as combat organizations, the 51st and 52d Defense Battalions, never saw combat. Instead, the "labor troops," the Marine depot and ammunition companies, and the officers' stewards were the ones who garnered the battle credits and took the casualties suffered by black Marines during the war. The Personnel Department at Headquarters Marine Corps in a postwar tabulation of casualties established that nine black Marines were killed in action or died of wounds, while 78 others were wounded in action and nine suffered from combat fatigue; 35 men died of other causes.[1] Inasmuch as the duties of the men in the depot and ammunition companies and those of the stewards were not supposed to bring them into direct confrontation with the Japanese, the casualty toll was not inconsiderable.

It was quite apparent to Marine planners in the early part of the war that the Marine Corps needed a vastly increased and improved supply system in the Pacific, one that could support the offensive thrust of hundreds of thousands of Marines. The need was felt not only at the rear and forward area support bases but in combat itself in the crucial area of shore party operations, the ship-to-shore movement of essential equipment and supplies. And once those supplies were ashore, they had to be stockpiled, shifted, sorted, and moved forward into the hands of the Marines battling the Japanese.

Gradually, an elaborate system did evolve which included base depots, which received, stored, processed, and shipped supplies of all sorts to combat units, and field depots, which were intended to be forward supply activities in operational areas. There were other organizations too, service and supply battalions, for instance, which performed these support activities for local base areas. All of these organizations were primarily composed of specialist companies which handled various types of supplies and equipment, salvaging and repairing non-expendable items where possible. What was missing at first was an essential element of the Marine logistical system, labor troops. All the vast assemblage of equipment had to be moved by ship and those ships had to be unloaded and reloaded time and again. The Marine Corps had no stevedores and found in its early combat operations that using combat troops for the unloading tasks was highly unsatisfactory. They were not doing the job for which they had been trained.

When the prospective number of black Marines was greatly increased in 1943, the problem of their employment arose. Headquarters Marine Corps began thinking about additional pioneer units, not the organic pioneer battalions of the Marine divisions, which were engineer organizations specializing in shore party operations, but units which would in effect serve as stevedores. The thousands of men destined for Montford Point were a ready-made manpower reservoir. Instead of organizing battalions or larger organizations, the Marine Corps formed the black Marines into company-sized units that could be deployed as soon as their ranks were filled from boot camp and shifted about more easily as the need for their services arose.

On 8 March 1943, the 1st Marine Depot Company was activated at Montford Point; its commander was Captain Jason M. Austin, Jr. Organized according to a table of organization approved less than a month before, the company included three officers and 110 enlisted men formed into a headquarters and two platoons and lightly armed with rifles, carbines, and submachine guns.[2] All but one of the 101 blacks in the company were privates; the other was an assistant cook, Ulysses J. Lucas. The nine NCOs in the company were white. Until enough black NCOs could be selected and

DEPOT AND AMMUNITION COMPANIES 1943-1946

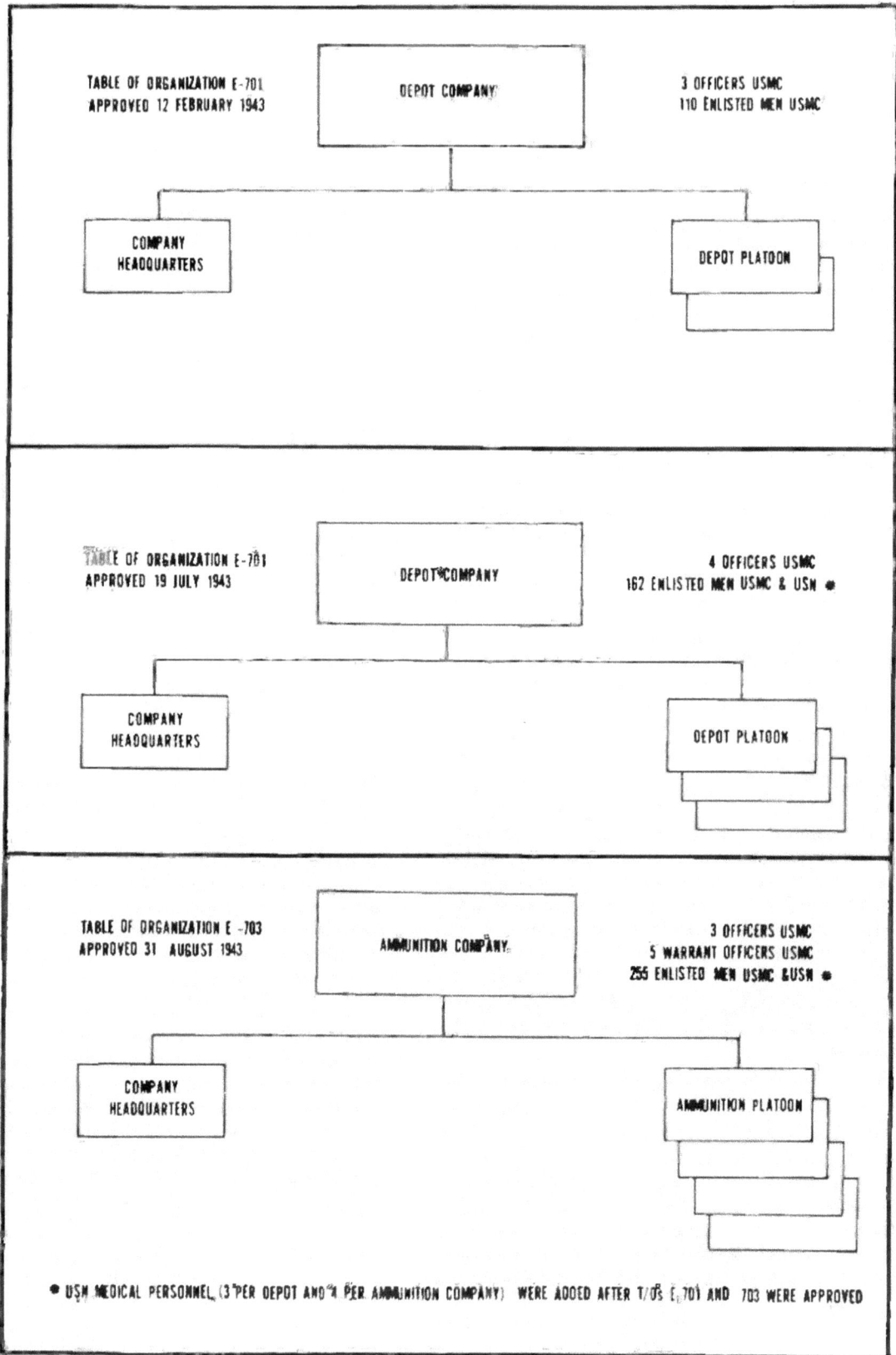

TABLE OF ORGANIZATION E-701
APPROVED 12 FEBRUARY 1943

DEPOT COMPANY

3 OFFICERS USMC
110 ENLISTED MEN USMC

COMPANY HEADQUARTERS

DEPOT PLATOON

TABLE OF ORGANIZATION E-701
APPROVED 19 JULY 1943

DEPOT COMPANY

4 OFFICERS USMC
162 ENLISTED MEN USMC & USN *

COMPANY HEADQUARTERS

DEPOT PLATOON

TABLE OF ORGANIZATION E-703
APPROVED 31 AUGUST 1943

AMMUNITION COMPANY

3 OFFICERS USMC
5 WARRANT OFFICERS USMC
255 ENLISTED MEN USMC & USN *

COMPANY HEADQUARTERS

AMMUNITION PLATOON

* USN MEDICAL PERSONNEL (3 PER DEPOT AND 4 PER AMMUNITION COMPANY) WERE ADDED AFTER T/O'S E-701 AND 703 WERE APPROVED

trained this was to be the pattern for the black Marine depot companies. Eventually, black NCOs moved up through the ranks replacing the whites who were transferred out to other organizations. On the whole, the first units to leave the States became all black below the officer level overseas. In 1944 and 1945 depot companies leaving Montford Point had black NCOs from first sergeant on down the line.

This policy of replacing white NCOs with blacks was in keeping with Letter of Instruction 421 which the Commandant issued on 14 March 1943. In the letter, in an attempt to avoid racial friction, General Holcomb stated that in no case would there be black NCOs senior to white men in the same unit and that it was desirable that few, if any, be of the same rank. The instructions specifically stated that it was not the intent of the letter to hinder promotion of blacks, in fact the Commandant indicated it was his aim that commanders exert every effort to locate blacks "having the requisite qualities of intelligence, education, and leadership to become noncommissioned officers." As an example he noted that if a black corporal was qualified for promotion to sergeant while there were still white corporals in his unit, he would be promoted but he would be transferred to a billet where his services could be used at the higher rank.[3] Although this letter to commanding officers was classified "Confidential," there was no doubt in the minds of most black Marines that such an order existed: they could see its dictums in operation. Still others saw the letter, including the sergeant major of the 51st Defense Battalion. He later remarked, in emphasizing that men of "intelligence, education, and leadership" had been found, that no black men in his office had a general classification test score of less than 110.[4]

After 10 depot companies had been formed and deployed in the period between March and September 1943, a new type of black unit came into being, the Marine ammunition company. Conceived of as a hard-working partner of the white ordnance companies in the base and field depots, the ammunition companies were to load and unload, sort and stack, manhandle and guard ammunition, moving it from ship to shore to dump, and in combat, forward to the frontline troops and firing batteries. The 1st Marine Ammunition Company was organized at Montford Point on 1 October 1943

with Second Lieutenant Placido A. Gomez in command.

Where the depot companies had a minimum of training before they shipped out, the ammunition companies usually spent at least two months at Montford Point before going overseas. The men were given familiarization courses on various types of ammunition and fuses, often practising moving ammunition containers from landing craft to inshore dumps. Some potential NCOs were sent to camouflage school and others were given special training in handling ammunition. The staff NCO billets in the companies went to white ordnance specialists, a condition that remained throughout the war. While the handling of ammunition required heavy labor, it also required experienced supervision to emphasize and enforce safety regulations.

The ammunition company was a large organization with a total strength of eight officers and 251 enlisted men. The unit was organized into a headquarters and four ammunition platoons with the men armed with rifles and carbines. Unlike the depot companies which had no organic transportation, the ammunition company rated a number of its own jeeps, trucks, and trailers.[5] The permanent complement of white line and specialist staff NCOs in the ammunition companies stifled Negro promotions to those ranks but the units operated effectively despite this. In the 3d Ammunition Company, one black veteran recalled: "The white NCOs we had was wonderful, a bunch of swell fellows. You couldn't go wrong with them . . . we were together; we worked as a team."[6]

From October 1943 until September 1944, one ammunition company and two depot companies were organized every month at Montford Point. The last of 12 ammunition companies was activated on 1 September 1944, the same day that the 33d and 34th Marine Depot Companies came into being. Depot companies continued to be formed, however, and 51 were organized, with the last four (the 46th, 47th, 48th, and 49th) activated on 1 October 1945 after the war was over. There were actually two 5th and 6th Marine Depot Companies; the first pair were sent out to New Caledonia in August 1943 to provide reinforcements for the four earlier depot companies when the addition of a third platoon to the table of organization brought each companies' total strength up to 163 officers and men.[7]

Into Service Overseas

A colorful description of the state of training of the depot companies before they shipped out was provided by the former first sergeant of one of them, who recalled:

> . . . there was no training these Negroes was doing, such as infantry training. The only training they had was what they had received at boot camp. And of course they did a hell of a lot of drilling. They were some of the drillingest people that you'd ever seen in your life.

From his point of view all the black depot company Marine needed "was a strong back," and "he already had that and so there was no need of training him because that was all he was going to do, to load and unload ships and haul ammunition and supplies into the line for the fighting troops." [8]

Like those depot units which followed it, the 1st Marine Depot Company did not spend much time at Montford Point once it had been formed. Three weeks after its organization, the company was on a train bound for the west coast. When the men arrived at San Diego on 5 April 1943, the Marine Corps base newspaper noted their arrival and reported: "after spending their first few hours squaring their gear, the men put on a warm-up demonstration of close order drill that left observers gaping." [9]

On 16 April, the company boarded ship, the destroyer USS *Hunt* (DD–674) and two days later sailed for Noumea on New Caledonia. This was the first of many such sailings from San Diego; other depot and ammunition companies left the States from San Francisco and Pleasanton in California, and Norfolk, Bayonne, and Davisville on the east coast, and from New Orleans and Gulf Port in the south, depending on where the shipping was available.

The destination of the 1st Marine Depot Company and of the next five companies to follow it was New Caledonia, where the 1st Base Depot was headquartered, its responsibility the support of Marine forces in the Solomons, where the campaign for Guadalcanal had just ended. In the same month that the 1st Marine Depot Company left the States, a new base depot, the 4th, was organized on New Caledonia, absorbing half the quartermaster personnel and taking the title to half the supplies stored in 1st Base Depot facilities. In May the new organization moved forward to the island of Banika in the Russell Group north of Guadalcanal to be in position to support Marine combat troops as they moved forward into the central and northern Solomons. [10] A number of black depot and ammunition companies were to serve in both base depots while the advance northward continued to its eventual culmination in mid-1944 with the encirclement and neutralization of the Japanese base at Rabaul on New Britain.

The value of the first depot company was immediately felt when it arrived at Noumea in May. Prior to this time, the shorthanded base depot had had to call on other Marine units for working parties, including convalescent wounded in mobile base hospitals, to augment ship loading and unloading details. The 1st Marine Depot Company was really welcome; "these troops offered the first solution to the depot's labor problem." [11] Other black Marine depot companies were soon on hand. The 2d and 3d Companies arrived together on 30 June, having been raised simultaneously at Montford Point in April, a pattern that applied to many pairs of depot companies which served together throughout the war.

The next company to come, the 4th, arrived alone in late July but did not stay long on New Caledonia. In concert with the earliest arrival, the 1st Depot Company, it boarded the transport USS *Crescent City* (AP–40) on 5 August and sailed north for Guadalcanal. Arriving in time on the 12th to be greeted with a harmless flyover by a Japanese pilot who had just finished attacking the island, the black Marines transhipped to smaller inter-island transports and left for Banika where they were to provide the first labor troops to join the 4th Base Depot. The two companies arrived 13 August and disembarked in a period of nightly air raids, got their first taste of a bombing raid on the 14th, and provided their first working parties on the docks on the 15th. [12]

After the initial movement of depot companies to New Caledonia and the Solomons to help support ongoing operations in the South and Southwest Pacific theatres, the next destination for many units was the Hawaiian Islands. The first pair to start that way were the 7th and 8th Marine Depot Companies, which arrived by way of Davisville, Rhode Island and the Panama Canal, with a stopover at Pago Pago in American Samoa, and a nine-month stint supporting operations in the Gilberts and Marshalls at the FMF Base Depot at Funafuti. By the time these companies finally arrived at Pearl Harbor in July 1944, a number of other depot and ammunition companies from Montford Point had already joined the 6th Base Depot on Oahu. Others were assigned to service and supply depots and battalions on other islands, like Hawaii, Maui, and Kauai, where Marine units trained and staged for Central Pacific operations. Two companies were sent down into the Marshalls, the 1st Marine Ammunition Company, which had a short stay at Kwajalein right after the atoll was taken in February before it returned to Oahu, and the 15th Marine Depot Company, which reached Allen Island at Kwajalein on 7 March and stayed there for the rest of the war.

Some of the units reporting to the Hawaiian Islands in the spring of 1944 were assigned to the 7th Field Depot: 3d Marine Ammunition Company and the 18th, 19th, and 20th Marine Depot Companies. Two ammunition companies, the 2d and 4th, were sent to Guadalcanal where they became part of the 5th Field Depot. These were destined to be the first black Marine units to take part in combat operations.

Combat in the Marianas

Saipan was the first target in the Marianas with D-Day 15 June 1944. The black Marines assigned to the 7th Field Depot helped load the supplies of the assault forces of the 2d and 4th Marine Divisions of the V Amphibious Corps. The two ammunition companies of 5th Field Depot on Guadalcanal performed similar duties for the 3d Marine Division and the 1st Provisional Marine Brigade of the III Amphibious Corps, which was slated to land in assault on Guam. In all cases the units were assigned to ship unloading details and to the shore parties of the assault echelons.

Elements of most of the black Marine units at Saipan got ashore on D-Day. A member of the 3d Marine Ammunition Company, Sergeant Ernest W. Coney, gave his version of the landing:

> Sixteen men were assigned to the ships' platoons and twenty-five to floating dumps [pontoon barges moored just off the reef's edge as transfer points]. The rest got ready to disembark at 0700. At 0600 it was bright enough to see an island dead ahead and smoke was pouring up from the earth as our planes was bombing and strafing. . . .
> We went over the side at 0700 and into the waiting landing boat. We shoved off toward the island and as usual we rode around in circles before going ashore. When we did start for the island, shells began to fall all

around us. We was given orders to turn around and get into an amphibious alligator 'cause we could not make it in—in the landing boat.
> We changed over and then waited . . . we hit the beach at 1400 and immediately started diggin' in because it seemed as though the Japs had gotten the range. One team had an amphibian tractor shot out from under it as it was being unloaded—miraculously all the men escaped without injury.[14]

Others were not as fortunate; PFC Leroy Seals of Brooklyn, New York was wounded a few hours after the landing and died the next day. Men from the company positioned near the beachhead perimeter helped repulse an enemy counterattack during the night of D-Day and were credited with knocking out a Japanese machine gun.

The depot companies were no less active on 15 June; most of the men of the 18th and 20th Companies landed in support of the 4th Marine Division while the 19th, which was part of the 2d Division's shore party, sweated cargo out of the holds and into landing craft for the trip to the fire-swept shore. One platoon of the 18th attached to the 3d Battalion, 23d Marines landed on Blue Beach 1, directly behind the town of Charan Kanoa, about two and a half hours after the assault wave had landed. As it disembarked, a mortar shell hit and exploded about 25 feet away. It caused four casualties (PFC Charles F. Smith and Privates Albert W. Sims, Jeff Smith, and Hayse Stewart) who were evacuated back to a transport. The platoon pushed inland to find cover from the enemy shelling. One squad was called up to replace riflemen in the front lines which were not more than 100 yards off the beach.

During the night, small enemy groups probed the left flank of the 23d Marines in the gap between that regiment and the 8th Marines to the north. Those who penetrated were mopped up by units in the rear, including the 18th Depot. When the line was stabilized, the 18th was pulled out to take over its normal duties of handling supplies. Of this period, the company commander, Captain William M. Barr, reported:

> Mortar shells were still raining down as my boys unloaded ammunition, demolition material, and other supplies from amphibious trucks. They set up "security" to keep out snipers as they helped load casualties aboard boats to go to hospital ships. Rifle fire was thick as they rode guard on trucks carrying high octane gasoline from the beach. A squad leader killed a Jap sniper that had crawled into a foxhole next to his. They stood waist deep in surf unloading boats as vital supplies of food and water were brought in . . . there

On D-Day at Saipan, black Marines pause at the beach's edge before receiving orders to move inland. (USMC Photo 83928).

were only a few scattered snipers on the beach. My boys accounted for several of these.[14]

A brief account of the D-Day experiences of the 20th Marine Depot Company reached the American press in the account of its commander, Captain William C. Adams:

> My company landed about 2 p.m. on D-Day [on Yellow Beach 2 supporting the 1st Battalion, 25th Marines]. We were the third wave, and all hell was breaking when we came in. It was still touch and go when we hit shore, and it took some time to establish a foothold.
> My men performed excellently. I had previously told them: "You are the first Negro troops ever to go into action in the Marine Corps. What you do with the situation that confronts you, and how you perform, will be the basis on which you, and your race, will be judged. . . .
> They did a swell job . . . Among my own company casualties, my orderly was killed. My men are still living in foxholes.[15]

The orderly was Private Kenneth J. Tibbs of Columbus, Ohio, who died of wounds on D-Day. He was the first black Marine fatality as the result of enemy action in World War II. The rest of the men in his company were not unmindful of the precarious situation on the beaches of Saipan and immediately took steps to improve their defenses. As Captain Adams noted: "they were very provident, and by the second day had all types of arms they had never been issued, such as . . . machine guns, and even .50 [caliber] machine guns." [16]

The 19th Marine Depot Company did not come ashore until 22 June and remained as part of the 2d Division shore party for five more days before it reverted to operational control of the 7th Field Depot. The 19th was a lucky outfit; it suffered no casualties on Saipan, nor was anyone hit when it took part in the Okinawa campaign nearly a year later. There were still other casualties in the Negro companies on Saipan, though, after the holocaust of D-Day. On 16 June, Private Willie J. Atkinson of the 18th Company was wounded and PFC Robert L. Neal of the ammunition company was shell-shocked and hospitalized. The next day PFC William B. Townsend of the 18th Company was hit. One of the officers of the 18th Company, Second Lieutenant Edmund C. Forehand, was wounded on the 21st, and PFC Lawrence Pellerin, Jr., of the 20th Company became a casualty the next day. As the fighting wore on into July, Corporal John S. Newsome of the 18th and Private Willie S. King of the 20th were wounded on the 4th, Private John S. Novy of the ammunition company was hit on the 9th, and the last black Marine casualty during the battle, Private Willie Travis Jr. of the 18th Company was wounded on the 13th.

The men in these four black companies were not the only black Marines on Saipan. The action was such that areas normally considered "safe" and "behind the lines" were subjected to enemy fire. During Japanese shelling that dropped in on the headquarters compound of the 2d Marine Division on 20 June, Cook 3d Class Timerlate E. Kirvin and Steward's Assistant 2d Class Samuel J. Love, Jr., both received leg wounds, thus earning the unwanted distinction of being the first Stewards' Branch combat casualties of the war.

The action of the black Marines under heavy fire and in a situation of unremitting toil and danger on Saipan did not go unnoticed at Headquarters Marine Corps or in the national press and news magazines. The Commandant, General Vandergrift, was quoted as saying: "The Negro Marines are no longer on trial. They are Marines, period." [17] Robert Sherrod, the war correspondent, reported in *Time*: "Negro Marines, under fire for the first time, have rated a universal 4.0 on Saipan." [18] In the naval efficiency rating system there could be no higher mark.

Indeed the black Marines had performed well under fire and the units of the 7th Field Depot that directly supported the 4th Marine Division, (3d Ammunition and 18th, 19th, and 20th Depot Companies) were included in the award of the Presidential Unit Citation given to that organization for its combat role on Saipan and Tinian. The latter island, close to Saipan, was taken in a classic shore-to-shore amphibious assault during the last week of July 1944. No black Marine casualties were incurred in the fighting, although elements of the 3d Ammunition Company did accompany the assault troops and the depot companies provided, as usual, loading and unloading support.

The last of the trio of operations in the Marianas was the recapture of Guam, lost to the Japanese in the early days of the war. The landing, originally set for 18 June 1944, was put off as a result of the heavy fighting on Saipan, and all the troops headed for the target were ship weary from their many weeks on transports when the actual landing was made on 21 July 1944. Just as eager as the rest to get ashore were the 2d and 4th Marine Ammunition Companies. Three platoons of the 2d were assigned to direct support of the 3d Marine Division landing on the Asan beachhead north of Orote Peninsula; the 4th Company, with the 4th Platoon of the 2d Company attached, was in direct support of the 1st Provisional Marine Brigade landing to the south of the peninsula at Agat.

A heavy naval bombardment, most intense of the war in the Pacific thus far, leveled most of the beach defenses of Guam, but there were still some antiboat guns operative and Japanese mortars and machine guns were active. The fire was particularly devastating on the 1st Brigade's beaches and in the waters offshore, and the black Marines were in the thick of it, unloading cargo from LSTs standing off the reef. The 3d Division had landed in a natural amphitheater with the Japanese holding the high ground overlooking the beaches. Considering the situation, the 2d Marine Ammunition Company was lucky to have only one man wounded, PFC Henry L. Jones, on 22 July.

On the night of D-Day, one of the platoons of the reinforced 4th Ammunition Company, which was guarding the brigade ammunition dump, intercepted and killed 14 Japanese soldiers laden with explosives. There were no casualties in this fire fight but a few days later (24 July) three men working on the beaches were wounded by fire from Japanese guns on Orote Peninsula: PFC Wilbert J. Webb and Privates Darnell Hayes and Jim W. Jones.

During the rest of the fighting on this island, the two companies continued to support the advancing Marines, reverting to operational control of the 5th Field Depot on 22 August, 12 days after the island was declared secure. The 4th Marine Ammunition Company and the 4th Platoon of the 2d Company were included in the Navy Unit Commendation awarded to the 1st Provisional Marine Brigade for its actions on Guam. The brigade com-

Men of the 3d Ammunition Company take a break during the fighting on Saipan. Seated on the Japanese bike is PFC Horace Boykin; seated (l to r) are Corporal Willis T. Anthony and PFCs Emmitt Shackelford and Eugene Purdy. (USMC Photo 86008).

mander, Brigadier General Lemuel C. Shepherd, Jr., wrote the 4th Company's commander, First Lieutenant Russell S. LaPointe, commending:

> . . . the splendid and expeditious manner in which supplies and equipment were unloaded from the LST's and LCT's of our Attack Group. Working long hours, frequently during nights, and in at least two instances under enemy fire . . . [you] so coordinated your unloading efforts as to keep supplies flowing to the beach. You have contributed in large measure to the successful and rapid movement of combat supplies in this amphibious operation.[19]

The end of the operation on Guam did not mean the end of encounters with the Japanese. Two men from the 4th Ammunition Com-

pany, PFCs George F. Gaines and Lawrence H. Hill, were wounded on 27 September by enemy troops. Some of the ammunition company men were particularly adept at hunting the stragglers down. One man, brought up in the Mississippi bayou country, who was a truck driver in Memphis when he joined the Marines, ran up quite a personal score. PFC Luther Woodward of the 4th Ammunition Company also earned the highest decoration won by a black Marine in World War II for a feat performed in December 1944. One afternoon, he saw some fresh footprints close to the ammunition dump he was guarding; he followed them through the thick brush to a native hut in a clearing, where he spotted six

Japanese. Opening fire, he killed one and wounded another before the survivors fled. Returning to camp, Woodward got five of his comrades to join him in hunting down the enemy and before they were through they had killed two more of the Japanese, one of them falling to Woodward's rifle. For his courage and initiative, he was decorated with the Bronze Star on 11 January 1945, an award subsequently upgraded to the Silver Star.[20]

Combat on Peleliu

The 11th Marine Depot Company, raised at Montford Point on 7 October 1943, had originally joined the 4th Base Depot on Banika when it went overseas in December, but in July 1944 it was transferred to Guadalcanal and joined the 16th Field Depot, which supported the 1st Marine Division. In August, the 7th Marine Ammunition Company, formed only four months before at Montford Point, arrived and also joined the 16th Depot. The two black Marine companies were destined to take part in the bloody battle for the island of Peleliu in the Palau Islands.

On the last day of August, the 1st Marine Division mounted out for the operation, and on 15 September its assault waves began landing on Peleliu in the face of heavy enemy fire. For the first few days, most of the black Marines served in ships' platoons unloading supplies for the run to the beaches, but soon, in small detachments, they began to come ashore to work in the dumps, to move supplies and ammunition to the front lines, and to help evacuate the wounded.

The fierceness of the Japanese resistance on the small island was soon attested to by the mounting toll of black casualties. The first black Marine wounded was Private Dyrel A. Shuler of the ammunition company, hit on 20 September. Two days later, the 11th Depot had its first casualty, Private Predell Hamblin. Then, on 23 and 24 September, eight of the depot company Marines were wounded by enemy fire: Corporal Clifford W. Stewart; PFCs Willie A. Rushton; Carleton Shanks, Jr.; Kenneth R. Stevens; Edward J. Swain; Bernard L. Warfield; and Earl L. Washington; and Private Joseph Williams. Two days later, six more men were wounded: Corporal Lawrence V. Cole; PFCs Irving A. Banks; Timothy Black; Paul B. Cook; Oscar A. Edmonds; and Edgar T. Grace. In October, two more men of

the 11th Depot Company were wounded, both on the 19th, Gunnery Sergeant Victor B. Kee and Private Everett Seals, giving the company the highest casualty rate of any black Marine unit in World War II.

The 7th Ammunition Company suffered the last black Marine casualties on Peleliu. Corporal Charles E. Cain was wounded on 9 October and Private John Copeland died of wounds received the same day. On the 26th, PFC James E. Moore was hit, and Private John Edmunds was wounded and evacuated on the last day of October.

The fighting on the island was as intense as any in the Pacific war and the two black Marine companies bore their share of the load. Even while the close combat was raging, Major General William H. Rupertus, commanding the 1st Division, wrote an identical letter of commendation to each of the commanding officers, which stated:

> 1. The performance of duty of the officers and men of your command has, throughout the landing on Peleliu and the assault phase, been such as to warrant the highest praise. Unit commanders have repeatedly brought to my attention the whole-hearted cooperation and untiring efforts exhibited by each individual.
> 2. The Negro race can well be proud of the work performed by the 7th Ammunition Company [11th Depot Company] as they have demonstrated in every respect that they appreciate the privilege of wearing a Marine uniform and serving with Marines in combat. Please convey to your command these sentiments and inform them that in the eyes of the entire Division they have earned a "Well Done."[21]

Combat on Iwo Jima

Black Marines were also present and accounted for at the largest all-Marine amphibious operation in the Pacific—Iwo Jima. Besides the Stewards' Branch personnel who served in all combat operations that the ammunition and depot companies took part in, the black Marines that landed on the small volcanic island were all members of the 8th Field Depot. As part of that unit they were cited with the rest of the support troops of the V Amphibious Corps in the Navy Unit Commendation awarded for their part in the furious month-long battle for Iwo Jima.

All four of the black Marine companies at Iwo were assigned to the V Corps shore party and two, the 8th Ammunition and 36th Depot, landed on D-Day, 19 February 1945. The soft,

Two black Marines take cover on the beach at Iwo Jima on D-Day while the shattered hulk of a DUKW smokes behind them. (USMC Photo 111123).

clinging volcanic sand and the almost constant enemy shellfire made life on the beaches a living hell, but the black Marines stuck to their jobs of unloading landing craft and amphibious vehicles. Amazingly, no one was hit for the first few days but then a steady attrition started.

On 22 February, a white officer, Second Lieutenant Francis J. DeLapp, and Corporal Gilman D. Brooks of the ammunition company were wounded. Three days later, PFC Sylvester J. Cobb from the same company was also wounded and Corporal Hubert E. Daverney and Private James M. Wilkins of the 34th Depot died of wounds received on the fire-swept beaches. Three other men from the 34th Company were hit on 25 February, Sergeant William L. Bowman, PFC Raymond Glenn, and Private James Hawthorne, Sr, as was a black Marine replacement, PFC William T. Bowen. The 34th Company's last casualty in February, PFC Henry L. Terry, was wounded the next day. The 33d and 34th Depot Companies had landed on 24 February after the men had served in ships' platoons getting supplies started on the way to the beach.

In early March the ammunition company suffered several more casualties. On the 2d, Private William L. Jackson was wounded and evacuated and PFC Melvin L. Thomas died of wounds. On 8 March, Private "J" "B" Saunders was wounded. As the fighting moved to the northern tip of the island the likelihood of further casualties in the black companies seemed remote. But the beleaguered Japanese had a painful surprise left for the Americans. Early on 26 March, 10 days after Iwo Jima was officially delcared secure, a well-armed column of 200-300 Japanese, including many officers and senior NCOs, slipped past the Marine infantrymen who had them holed up near the northernmost airfield and launched a full-scale attack on the Army and Marine troops camped near the western beaches. The units struck included elements of the Corps Shore Party, the 5th Pioneer Battalion, Army Air Forces squadrons, and an Army antiaircraft artillery battalion. The action was wild and furious in the dark; it was hard to tell friend from foe since many Japanese were armed with American weapons.[22] The black Marines were in the thick of the fighting and took part in the mop-up of the enemy remnants at daylight. Two members of the 36th Marine Depot Company, Privates James M. Whitlock and James

Davis, both received Bronze Star Medals for "heroic achievement in connection with operations against the enemy."[23]

There was a cost too for the black Marines. PFC Harold Smith of the 8th Ammunition Company died of wounds received in the fighting; Corporals Richard M. Bowen and Warren J. McDaughtery were wounded but survived. The 36th Depot Company lost Private Vardell Donaldson who succumbed to his wounds, but PFC Charles Davis and Private Miles Worth recovered from their injuries.

The Commander, Corps Shore Party, Colonel Leland S. Swindler, who was also commander of the 8th Field Depot, was particularly pleased with the actions of the black Marines in this battle and in his report for Iwo Jima stated that he was:

> . . . highly gratified with the performance of these colored troops, whose normal function is that of labor troops, while in direct contact with the enemy for the first time. Proper security prevented their being taken unaware, and they conducted themselves with marked coolness and courage. Careful investigation shows that they displayed modesty in reporting their own part in the action.[24]

Once the fighting was over, the units of the 8th Field Depot returned to Hilo in the Hawaiian Islands to prepare for the next operation. The rear echelons of the four black companies, which had moved forward to Saipan while the main bodies were on Iwo, now rejoined. The next deployment of the 8th Field Depot would have been during the invasion of Japan, but the ending of the war made it occupation duty instead.

Combat on Okinawa

The largest number of black Marines to serve in combat took part in the seizure of Okinawa in the Ryukyu Islands, the last Japanese bastion to fall before the atomic bomb and the threat of invasion of the home islands combined to bring the war to an end. Three ammunition companies, the 1st, 3d, and 12th, and four depot companies, the 5th, 18th, 37th, and 38th, of the 7th Field Depot arrived at Okinawa on D-Day, 1 April 1945. Later in the month, the 20th Marine Depot Company came in from Saipan and in May the 9th and 10th Companies arrived from Guadalcanal and the 19th from Saipan.

The black Marines on the attack transport USS *Bladen* (APA-63), the 1st and 3d Ammunition Companies, the 5th Depot Company, and part of the 38th Depot, and those on the USS *Berrien* (APA-62), the rest of the 38th and part of the 37th Depot, took part in the 2d Marine Division demonstration landing off the southeast coast of Okinawa. At the same time the assault troops of the Tenth Army (III Amphibious Corps and the Army's XXIV Corps) went ashore on the western coast at the narrow waist of the 60-mile-long island. In the feint attack, the men climbed into landing craft, rendezvoused, formed assault waves, and roared in toward the beach, turning around 500 yards from the shoreline.[25] The next day this maneuver was repeated in hope that it would prevent the Japanese commander from moving troops north to oppose the actual landings.

On 3 April, most of the black Marines landed on the island, ready to support the 1st and 6th Marine Divisions, the assault troops of the III Corps. Unlike previous landings in which the depot and ammunition companies had been involved, there was little opposition on the beaches or in the first days ashore in the Marines' operational area, the northern two-thirds of the island. The Japanese had concentrated their defenses on the south, but there was more than enough action in the north to keep everyone in III Corps busy before the two Marine divisions moved south to join the main battle. Japanese air raids were frequent, mostly aimed at the cluster of ships offshore, and the barrier of antiaircraft fire thrown up loosed a deadly shower of shell fragments that often fell on the troops near the beaches.

Many of the casualties suffered by the black units occurred in April, when their camps and work areas were still relatively near the front lines. The 5th Marine Depot Company had

Three Marines of the 34th Depot Company on the beach at Iwo Jima. (l to r) PFCs Willie J. Kanady, Eugene F. Hill, and Joe Alexander. (USMC Photo 113835).

three men wounded. PFC Willie Hampton on the 6th, Private Therrance J. Mercier on the 15th, and Private Eldridge O. Oliver on the 28th. The 1st Ammunition Company had two men wounded, PFC Thomas Early on the 10th and PFC Joshua Nickens on the 15th. The 3d Marine Ammunition Company, veteran of the Saipan and Tinian operations, suffered one of its last casualties of the war when Private Clifford Bryant was also wounded on 15 April. The 38th Depot Company had one man wounded, PFC Alvin A. Fitzpatrick, on 27 April. One of the blacks assigned to the officers' mess of the 29th Marines, Steward's Assistant 1st Class Joe N. Bryant, was wounded on 5 April, and in the 1st Marine Division's headquarters, Steward's Assistant 2d Class Ralph Woodkins caught a shell fragment in his face on 12 April.

Once the Tenth Army started to drive south with its two corps abreast striking against the deeply dug-in Japanese, the black labor troops had formidable transportation problems. Distances to the front lines lengthened and the roads turned into quagmires when the spring rains began to fall in torrential proportions. Carrying parties had to be organized to get supplies and ammunition to the troops and bring the casualties out of the forward areas. The black Marines of the depot and ammunition companies struggled with heavy and vital loads going both ways. Casualties were scattered, but continued to occur. Private Arthur Bowman, Jr., of the 12th Ammunition Company and Private Charles L. Burton of the 3d Ammunition Company were wounded in May and PFC Clarence H. Jackson of 3d Ammunition and PFC Richard E. Hines of 10th Depot in June.

The stewards in corps, wing, division, and regimental headquarters, some of whom volunteered as stretcher bearers when the fighting was heaviest, did not escape unscathed. Steward 2d Class Warren N. McGrew, Jr., was killed and shell fragments wounded Steward's Assistant 3d Class Willie Crenshaw of the 1st Division on 9 May and four days later two men in the 6th Division, Cook 3d Class Horace D. Holder and Steward's Assistant 3d Class Norman "B" Davis, were both struck in the same fashion. On 26 May, three stewards on the 29th Marines headquarters, Steward's Assistant 1st Class Joe N. Bryant, Steward's Assistant 3d Class Jerome Caffey, and Private Morris E. Clark, were all wounded; Bryant's second

wound in the campaign gave him an unsought-after "first" among black Marines. On the whole, however, considering the fury and length of the battle, the black Marines were lucky to have suffered so few casualties out of the more than 2,000 Montford Point men who served on Okinawa.

When the island was declared secure on 22 June 1945, there was little let-up in the workload of the black service troops. Okinawa was to be the principal supply and staging area for the invasion of Japan. Ships arrived continuously and supply dumps expanded to enormous proportions. When the war ended in mid-August, the thrust of preparations turned to occupation duty not only in Japan but in North China, where Marines were to help repatriate the Japanese troops and civilians in Hopeh and Shantung Provinces. Some of the black units that had served in the Okinawa operation would go forward to North China which was the objective of the III Amphibious Corps; others would remain on the island to help support the occupation effort. Similarly,

Men of the 12th Ammunition Company rest at the base of a Japanese Memorial on Okinawa during the drive to the north in April; on the steps (l to r), PFC Floyd O. Snowdon, Sr., and Pharmacist's Mate 2d class James R. Martin, on the monument (l to r), Privates John T. Walton, and Robison T. Ellingburg, PFC Clyde Brown and Private Robert Brawner. (USMC Photo 117624).

some of the Marine depot and ammunition companies that had served on Iwo Jima would accompany the V Amphibious Corps to Kyushu, the Japanese home island choosen as the objective for Marine occupying forces.

Occupation Duty[26]

The Sixth Army, which had been destined to make the assault on Kyushu if the war had continued, now provided the occupation troops for the seizure of southern Japan. As part of that army, the V Amphibious Corps would occupy Kyushu and southern Honshu with the 2d and 5th Marine Divisions and the Army's 32d Infantry Division. Speculation about how the Japanese would receive the Americans was rife in late August. Would some diehards ignore the Emperor's orders to lay down all arms? The swift and bloodless occupation of Yokusuka naval base on Tokyo Bay by the reinforced 4th Marines on 30 August provided the answer. The Japanese were fully prepared to cooperate.

The V Corps could now plan for administrative landings rather than the show of force once thought necessary. Corps headquarters and service troops and the 5th Marine Division mounted out from the Hawaiian Islands in late August and early September. The black Marines, now part of the 8th Service Regiment (redesignated on 1 June from the 8th Field Depot), moved forward with the corps troops in a variety of transports and landing ships. The convoy paused at Saipan to pick up the 2d Marine Division. The objective of the 5th Division and Corps Headquarters was the Japanese Naval base at Sasebo on the northwest coast of Kyushu; the 2d Division would initially occupy Nagasaki, 30 miles to the south. Once the entry ports were secure, the Marines, and the Army troops to come up later on turn-around shipping, would spread out all over the large island with its population of 10,000,000 people.

Three ammunition companies, the 6th, 8th, and 10th, made the voyage to Japan together with the 24th, 33d, 34th, 42d, and 43d Depot Companies. All arrived and disembarked at Sasebo between 22 and 26 September. The 36th Marine Depot Company came up to Sasebo in late October with the rear echelon of the 8th Service Regiment. The duties of the black Marines were not onerous and certainly did not compare with the intense activity of a combat operation. The dangerous task of disposing of Japanese explosives was handled by the Japanese themselves with minimal American involvement.

The stay in Japan was not a long one. The need for strong, reinforced combat forces became less and less apparent as time wore on with nothing but cooperation from the Japanese. The demobilization pressure from the States was strong and there were thousands of men in the V Corps with enough points for discharge when the word came that the 5th Marine Division would return home in December. The low point men of the 5th Division shifted to the 2d Division which would remain in Japan, and the high point men of the 2d joined the 5th Division for the homeward voyage.

The same reductions in force and transfers were taking place among the black Marine units. The 24th Depot Company was disbanded at Nagasaki on 15 November and a month later the 6th Ammunition Company passed out of existence at Sasebo. In both cases the men were transferred to units remaining in Japan or destined for service on Guam. In early January, the 8th Ammunition Company and the 33d, 34th, and 36th Depot Companies set sail for Guam to join the 5th Service Depot (formerly the 5th Field Depot). The 33d and 34th Companies were disbanded on Guam before the month was out. The 36th Depot Company stayed in existence a few months longer, making it back to Montford Point via San Francisco for disbandment on 17 June 1946. The 8th Ammunition Company, destined to be the last of its type to serve on active duty, stayed on Guam.

In Japan, the end of black Marine involvement in occupation duties was in sight. Except for a few stewards whose number was dwindling as demobilization took its toll, the last organized black units were slated to go. The 42d and 43d Depot Companies, which had been raised together at Montford Point on 14 March 1945, were disbanded exactly one year later at Sasebo. All those men eligible for discharge were transferred to the 10th Ammunition Company and those who still had time to serve were transferred to the 6th Service Depot in Hawaii. The last black Marine unit in Japan, the 10th Ammunition Company, boarded the merchant marine transport SS *Dashing Wave* on 5 April 1946 bound for San Diego. A month later at Montford Point the company was disbanded.

The experience of the black Marines who went to North China was quite similar to that of the men who served in Japan. The 7th Service Regiment (old 7th Field Depot) would support the III Amphibious Corps and have most of its men serving in the Tientsin area of Hopeh Province with corps headquarters and the 1st Marine Division. Two companies, 12th Ammunition and 20th Depot, would help support the 6th Marine Division at Tsingtao in Shantung Province. The mission of III Corps was to repatriate the Japanese troops and civilians in North China and to try to keep from getting involved in the civil war raging between the Chinese Nationalists and Communists. Since the U.S. Government recognized and supported the Nationalists as the legitimate government of China, the chances for peaceful accommodations with the Communists were slim. So there was always the chance of an ambush or some shots fired by a hidden sniper at Marines on guard or convoy duty.

The 1st Ammunition Company and the 5th, 37th, and 38th Depot Companies all left Okinawa with the III Corps-1st Division convoy in late September 1945, moving through mine-strewn waters and stormy weather to reach the anchorage off the Hai River which led to Tientsin. On the 30th, the 1st Ammunition and 38th Depot Companies went ashore with the first troops to land at Tangku, the port town for Tientsin. The other companies landed a few days later and all found their way to Tientsin.

The initial reception of the black Marines by the Chinese was a wary one. One of the black first sergeants recalled:

> We were moving down the street after we got to Tientsin, we were going down to the Melchior Building, and the Chinese would run out and touch a Marine on the face because they were very black, we had been out in the sun for a long time, and rub their hands on their face and see if it would come off, like they thought it was painted or something.
> . . . And they stayed clear of the Negroes, wouldn't have nothing to do with them for about a week. But soon as they found that this paint wouldn't come off, or what they thought was paint, I couldn't hardly separate [them] and had hell keeping them out of the barracks. They got to be very charming and very lovely.[27]

Like their counterparts in Japan, the black Marines in North China found that most heavy labor was performed by Orientals. A good part of the black companies' tasks consisted of guard duty both in Tientsin and Tangku and on the trains, landing craft, and trucks which ran the 30 miles between the two. Liberty was good, but segregation was the order of the day in China as it was in Japan and black and white Marines tended to congregate in their own special haunts.

The repatriation mission was handled with dispatch and hundreds of thousands of Japanese were sent home in the first few months the Marines were in China. The 1st Division, however, got involved in an unexpected task, guarding coal mines, trains, bridges, and rail lines from Communist attacks to ensure that coal would reach the city of Shanghai, which depended on Hopeh's mines to keep its factories and utilities running. This meant that the division would at least remain in China through the winter until the Nationalists could be persuaded to take over the guard duties. The need for many of the reinforced units of III Corps was greatly lessened and troop strength was cut drastically.

In January 1946, following the pattern prevalent throughout North China as demobilization measures accelerated, the low point men of the black companies transferred to the units that were to remain and those eligible for discharge joined the units going home. The 5th Depot and 1st Ammunition Companies boarded ship, the attack transport USS *Bolivar* (APA-34), on 7 January after being lightered from the docks at Tangku to the anchorage off the Hai River mouth. The *Bolivar* sailed south to Tsingtao and picked up the homeward-bound 20th Depot Company. The three units stayed together through San Diego and Camp Pendleton, where the west coast Marines remained to be processed for discharge, and the rest of the men entrained for Montford Point. On 21 February 1946, the trio of companies was disbanded at the camp where they had started their wartime careers.

The 37th and 38th Depot Companies left Tangku on 2 March, the same day that the 12th Ammunition Company cleared Tsingtao, ending the tour of black Marine units in North China. The two ships carrying the black troops reached San Diego a few days apart because the ammunition company stopped over at Pearl Harbor to transfer low point men and regulars to the 6th Service Depot. The journey onward to Montford Point ended in early April, where on the 2d the depot companies disbanded and on the 5th the ammunition company followed suit. With the exception of the 8th Ammunition Company, still on Guam, all of the black units that had taken part in the occupation of Japan and North China were gone.

Windup in the Pacific

Only seven of the 12 ammunition companies and 12 of the 51 depot companies raised during the war saw combat. For the rest, the war must have been as frustrating as it was for the two black defense battalions, but those troops at least had the satisfaction of knowing that they were trained for combat and might eventually take part in the fighting. With the labor companies there was only the satisfaction of doing their job well with just an outside chance that they might be tapped for battle. In the meantime, their job was to toil away at the essential but largely unrecognized or rewarded labor tasks that kept the supply channels filled to the combat echelons of the Marine Corps. In the 4th Service Depot on Banika, the 5th on Guam, and the 6th on Oahu and in the service and supply battalions on other islands, the routine was unending, 12-hour work days, six-day work weeks, with both periods lengthening when the schedule was stepped up to support new operations in forward areas.

The Hawaiian Islands at least had a tradition of multi-racial living and tolerance that softened the continued existence of segregation of blacks and whites in the services. The islands had towns and cities for liberty, places to go when time could be found. And the combat troops that rested and retrained there between operations had seen black Marines under fire on the beaches and knew that they had proved their mettle. Yet, there were continued reminders of the second-class status of blacks, racial slurs that were a reflection overseas of the situation at home. Some black Marines took the situation in stride, not expecting drastic change but seeing a gradual improvement in their status; other seethed with resentment at any unequal treatment, actual or imagined.

On Guam, which was very much a forward staging and supply area with few of the amenities that could be found in Hawaii, the inter-racial situation grew tense after the battle for the island was over. Yet, when a series of racial incidents flared up in December 1944, the black Marines were only peripherally involved. It is apparent when one reviews the lengthy 1,200-page report of the Court of Inquiry which resulted that the principal antagonists were white Marines and black sailors and that the black Marines generally kept to themselves and clear of entanglements.[28]

On the side of the blacks there was evidence that some white Marines, mainly members of the 3d Marine Division, were harassing individual blacks, shouting racial epithets, throwing stones and even, on occasion, smoke grenades into black encampments as they raced by in trucks. There was an apparent move to scare blacks away from Agana, the island capital, and make it, and the native women who lived there, a white preserve. In return, some blacks tended to act against individual whites when they had a chance, responding in kind with name calling and missiles. By mid-December 1944, the situation had grown serious enough in the eyes of the Island Command's Provost Marshal, Marine Colonel Benjamin A. Atkinson, for him to recommend to the island commander, Major General Henry L. Larsen, that he issue a general order on racial discrimination which was published on the 18th, stating:

> The present war has called together in our services men of many origins and various races and colors. All are presumed to be imbued with common ideals and standards. All wear the uniform of the United States. All are entitled to the respect to which that common service is entitled. There shall be no discrimination by reason of sectional birth, race, religion, or political beliefs. On the other hand, all individuals are charged with the responsibility of conducting themselves as becomes Americans.[29]

The sentiments were lofty, and certainly a truer reflection of the general's attitude than the famous remarks attributed to him at Montford Point in 1943. As the Court of Inquiry found, the general order was backed up by a serious intent to find and punish anyone who was indentified as a racial troublemaker. The order had little chance to take effect, however, before there was a series of shootings in and around Agana. In one, on 24 December, an off-duty white Marine MP fired on some blacks in the town without hitting anyone; more seriously, a white sailor shot and killed a black Marine of the 25th Depot Company in an argument over a native woman and a 27th Depot Company sentry shot a white Marine, who later died, who had harassed him on his post. Both men were convicted of voluntary manslaughter in subsequent trials.

The sum result of these incidents was that two truckloads of black sailors, labor troops from the island's Naval Supply Depot, mistakenly believing the dead black to be one of their own men, roared into Agana to a confrontation with outnumbered Marine MPs. Nothing serious happened this time, but on Christmas Day there was a virtual repetition of this incident, which resulted in the arrest of 43 black sailors, who proved to be armed with an assortment of stolen pistols, knives, and other weapons. That night Marine MPs patrolling the roads adjacent to the black sailors' encampment were fired on and one man was hit. A shakedown of the black companies tents the following morning revealed a number of illegal weapons hidden away in the tents, some of them stolen from the supply depot armory.

General Larsen immediately convened a Court of Inquiry to investigate the circumstances attending "the unlawful assembly and riot." As president of the court he appointed Colonel Samuel A. Woods, Jr., the man who had organized Montford Point Camp. By happenstance, Mr. Walter W. White, Executive Secretary of the National Association for the Advancement of Colored People, was in the central Pacific on a visit and he came to Guam when he heard of the trouble. He made his own investigation of the series of incidents with the help of the Navy and eventually ended up as counsel for several of the black sailors involved in the abortive affray in Agana.

The month-long hearings ranged far beyond the actual events to examine the state of morale of black troops on Guam and the background of racial incidents. The board in its findings reported that there was no evidence of organized racial prejudice on the island, a point in which Mr. White concurred. The board did recommend, however, that the black sailors who had been arrested in Agana be tried for unlawful assembly and rioting. It also recommended that several white Marines who had been apprehended for harassing blacks be court martialled. This was later done and all accused, black and white, were convicted and received varying sentences according to the gravity of their offenses under military law.

As part of the hearings, several black Marines from the 2d and 4th Ammunition Companies were called as witnesses to testify as to the state of morale of their own units and their own experiences with racial prejudice on Guam. Their responses indicated that the

Marine companies, in contrast to the Navy labor companies from which the accused blacks had come, were well disciplined and had had only scattered experience with racial incidents. One sergeant, Walter Averiett of the 2d Company, ascribed the relatively recent rash of racial name calling to replacements who had joined the 3d Marine Division since the seizure of Guam, pointing out that the black Marines had gotten "along well with old Third Marines, the fellows who hit the island, the ones who were here before being shipped home." [30] One fact that did obviously rankle the black Marines though was that blacks could not advance to line staff NCO rank in ammunition companies because these billets were held by white Marines. And it did not sit well with them either that the one black staff NCO in their companies, the mess sergeant, was not quartered with the other staff sergeants.

The so-called "Third Battle of Guam" was a minor *cause celebre* for a time, but it faded into the backwash of the war as the fighting came to a conclusion at Okinawa. Like other Marine units, the depot and ammunition companies were scheduled for return from the Pacific or disbandment as the requirement for their services lessened. There was a constant interchange of low point men with high point veterans as some companies left for home and others remained for a time overseas. The 4th Marine Depot Company was disbanded on Guam on 31 October 1945, the first such unit to go out of existence. The first three depot companies to go overseas returned together from Banika on the light cruiser *St. Louis* (CL-49) in December, disbanding at Montford Point on 4 January 1946. The first of the ammunition companies to disappear was the 6th which stood down in Sasebo on 15 December 1945. On 20 January, the 2d Ammunition Company disbanded on Guam and a month later (21 February) the 1st Ammunition Company was disbanded at Montford Point, followed five days later by the 3d Company.

In the early days of 1946, the rush to get the veterans qualified for discharge home used every conceivable type of Navy ship. Some black units returned to the States on escort carriers, some on cruisers, others on transports and cargo vessels. The routine was much the same in most cases, a stopover in California at Camp Pendleton to drop off those men being discharged on the west coast and a cross-country train trip for the rest to Montford Point and discharge there.

By mid-summer all but a few of the depot and ammunition companies had gone out of existence. On Oahu the sole remaining units were the 47th Depot Company and the 3d Platoon, 8th Ammunition Company, redesignated from a similar unit of the 11th Ammunition Company. This platoon, stationed at the Naval Ammunition Depot, Makaha Valley, was initially commanded by a black Marine, Platoon Sergeant Agrippa W. Smith, before a white officer was detailed to the task. On Guam the rest of the 8th Ammunition Company and the 49th Depot Company were all that remained of the units formed during and immediately after the war.

On 31 October 1946, the 47th Depot Company, now down to a strength of one officer, 18 black Marines and two black Navy medical corpsmen, was disbanded. In November, the ammunition platoon at Makaha Valley boarded ship for Guam and was disbanded there on its arrival on the 25th, its 80 men being absorbed by the parent 8th Ammunition Company. Eleven months later, on 30 September 1947, both the 8th and 49th Companies were deactivated and their men were transferred to the Headquarters and Service and Depot Support Companies of the 5th Service Depot; the latter company was a postwar organization designated as a black unit of the FMF.

Despite the unglamorous nature of the work they performed, the ammunition and depot companies of World War II helped make the reputation of black Marines, setting a high standard of discipline and combat effectiveness. The men, in common with most black servicemen during the war, suffered many personal slights as a result of segregation practices both in the States and overseas, but these shared adversities had the effect of bringing them closer together both as blacks and as Marines. When, in later years, an organization composed primarily of black Marine veterans was formed, its first president, Master Gunnery Sergeant Brooks E. Gray, Jr., would note: "There was much pride mixed with bitterness, in all of us at Montford Point during World War II. Real, as well as imagined, injustices were with us daily in those segregated units." But this situation "sparked a fierce determination to excel," and, he observed: "We represented the break-through of the final barrier in the American military by being part of the elite corps. . . ."[31]

Officials of the Montford Point Marine Association at their 1971 convention in New Orleans, (l to r) Sergeant Major Gilbert H. "Hashmark" Johnson, USMC (Ret.), Master Gunnery Sergeant Brooks E. Gray, Jr., USMC, Mr. William Hill, and Dr. Leonard L. Burns. (Photo courtesy of Dr. Burns).

For the depot and ammunition company veterans, this attitude of pride in having been successful Marines, in having done the job they were given to do and done it well, overrode other memories. The seemingly endless hours sweating in ships' holds, moving heavy loads across beaches and piers of a hundred islands, and stocking and sorting tons of supplies in a succession of dreary dumps had the virtue of toughening the men both physically and mentally. Looking back on it all, one veteran of the 3d Ammunition Company, Robert D. Little, summed up his, and others, feelings when he said: "If I had to do it all over again, I'd still be a black Marine . . . . I think they made a man of me."[32]

CHAPTER 5

BETWEEN THE WARS

Before the troop reductions and unit disbandments occurred overseas at the end of World War II, Montford Point Camp itself had some changes after the majority of black Marines had been dispatched to field duties. In October 1944 three of the then seven training companies of the Recruit Depot Battalion were disbanded and the Stewards' Branch Battalion was reduced to company strength. By that time there were 15,131 blacks in the Corps out of a total strength of approximately 475,000 men and women. Obviously, the black figure did not represent the 10 percent of Marine Corps strength that was contemplated in 1943, but the corps was never able to fill its black selective service quotas. In fact, only about 65 percent of the men called for induction were taken.[1]

In contrast, however, and encouragingly, 1944 saw the first signs that the Marine Corps would eventually have black officers. That summer the first black Marines were assigned to the Navy's V-12 program, which was designed to provide qualified enlisted men with a college education at selected colleges and universities and ultimately with a commission in the Navy or Marine Corps Reserve. Only a few months before, in April, Headquarters Marine Corps had made a study that recommended that no black Marine officers be procured at that time, but the study group recognized that such procurement might be ordered by higher authority, which led to recommendations, among others, that black officers be assigned to Montford Point only and that they not be assigned to command over white officers or enlisted men.[2]

This study was overtaken by events and the inevitability of the advent of black officers was recognized at Headquarters Marine Corps. Preparations were made to send two black college graduates, Charles F. Anderson, sergeant major of Montford Point Camp, and Charles W. Simmons, former sergeant major of the 51st Defense Battalion, to Quantico to the 9th Platoon Commanders Class.[3] To this original duo, one more college graduate was added, First Sergeant George F. Ellis, Jr., who had served overseas with the 26th Marine Depot Company. A rousing send-off party was held at the Staff NCO Club at Montford Point on 12 March 1945 to speed the officer candidates on their way to Quantico.[4] The letdown was tremendous when all three men failed to make the grade and receive their commissions; one was given a medical discharge for a congenital heart murmur, the other two failed to maintain the required military and scholastic rating, becoming a part of the 13 percent of the class that was not commissioned.[5] The bad news did not sit well with black Marines, and, as the new

First black Marine officer, Frederick C. Branch, has his second lieutenant's bars pinned on by his wife on 10 November 1945. (USMC Photo 5000-13).

sergeant major at Montford Point, Gilbert "Hashmark" Johnson, put it: "There were a number of questions asked and quite a bit of consternation." [6]

The questions were not without foundation, for the three men were among the best educated and militarily successful black Marines. Later in civilian life they became a lawyer (Anderson), a physician (Ellis), and a college professor and author (Simmons). They were followed in officers training by three similarly qualified black candidates who also failed to make the grade. [7]

But the inevitable did happen. Five more black Marines were assigned to the 16th Platoon Commanders Class meeting that summer at Quantico. This class was in training on V-J Day, and the members were given the opportunity to be discharged, to revert to regular enlisted status, or to stay on in abbreviated training and go on inactive duty as soon as they were commissioned. Of the five blacks one, PFC Frederick C. Branch, born in Hamlet, N.C. and formerly of the 51st Defense Battalion, elected to stay in the training course. Appropriately, on the Marine Corps birthday, 10 November 1945, Second Lieutenant Branch was commissioned as a reserve officer, the first black man to achieve this distinction. Although he immediately went on inactive duty, Branch stayed active in the reserve, commanding a black volunteer reserve unit in Philadelphia in 1949, and returned to active service during the Korean War.

In 1946, three black Marines who had been enrolled in the V-12 program were commissioned as reserve officers on inactive status: Charles C. Johnson of Washington, D.C.; Judd B. Davis of Fuquay Springs, North Carolina; and Herbert L. Brewer of San Antonio, Texas. Lieutenant Johnson resigned to accept a commission in the U.S. Public Health Service in November 1947; Lieutenant Davis was recalled to active duty during the Korean War but was found physically disqualified and was honorably discharged for physical reasons in 1952; Lieutenant Brewer served on active duty in the Korean War and in 1973 was a reserve colonel in the Philadelphia area, the highest ranking black officer in the Marine Corps Reserve.

In a sense, with those first commissions the ice had been broken, but the Marine Corps was still segregated when the war emergency ended and was to remain so for another four years. Montford Point Camp was still home base to all black Marines and the focal point of all comings and goings.

Colonel Herbert L. Brewer, originally commissioned in 1948, the highest ranking black officer in the Marine Corps Reserve in 1973. (USMC Photo A619582).

In all, 19,168 blacks had served in the Marine Corps in World War II and 12,738 of these men had served overseas. [8] The others were part of the training base at Montford Point or had done duty at the Marine Barracks, Naval Ammunition Depot, McAlester, Oklahoma, in depot units attached to the supply activities at Philadelphia and Norfolk, and in stewards' detachments at major posts and stations in the United States.

The rapid demobilization of the Marine Corps in late 1945 and 1946 created a time of considerable upheaval at Montford Point, a condition shared at most Marine Corps bases. The emphasis was on getting the men who were eligible out of service, and the 2d Casual Company at Montford Point, which processed most of the men, was handling an average of well over a thousand men a month in the first six months of 1946, reaching its peaks in February (1,945) and May (1,848). All recruit training of World War II lineage came to an end after 25 January 1946 when the 62 men in the last three recruit platoons, the 573d, 574th, and 575th, fired for record at the range at Stone Bay. The field sergeant major was Gunnery Sergeant Haywood D. Collier and the DIs of the final platoon, the 575th, were Corporal Charles E. Counts and PFC John A. Peeples, Jr.[9]

By January 1946, most black veterans had some idea of the shape of the postwar Marine Corps insofar as blacks were concerned. Separate and segregated units would continue, probably an antiaircraft battalion, some depot companies, the Stewards' Branch, and a small detachment at Montford Point. The prospect did not seem to have much appeal to the lower ranking black Marines.[10] Although a number of staff NCOs switched to the regular Marine Corps as career men, only a trickle of PFCs, corporals, and sergeants reenlisted. Apparently, in the rush for discharge and the resultant disbandment and consolidation of organized units, there did not appear to be much consistent purpose in what was going on at Montford Point. Topping this for many blacks was the continued segregation in the Corps and the fact that many of them waiting for discharge at Montford Point found themselves being used on work details in other parts of Camp Lejeune, cleaning up barracks and grounds occupied by white Marines. Naturally enough, this did not sit well with the young blacks, who were certain that the reverse situation would not apply.[11]

Deliberations at Headquarters Marine Corps regarding the postwar status of black Marines in the spring of 1946 were spurred on by Navy Department pronouncements of a policy of non-discrimination by reason of color or race in the naval service. A Bureau of Naval Personnel circular letter of 27 February announced the abolition of all restrictions in the Navy governing types of assignments in all ratings, in all activities, and on all ships. However, there was to be a 10 percent limitation on the number of blacks in any ship or activity.[12] An Army study group's report on postwar plans for black soldiers, issued in March, was more traditional in nature. The group recommended the retention of separate black units no larger than infantry regiments. Units were to be of all types, both combat and service, with a ratio one black to 10 whites throughout the Army.[13]

In the Marine Corps, which was contemplating an overall postwar strength of 100,000, the proportion of blacks was to be much lower than in the other services. There was a much diminished peacetime requirement for the types of units in which blacks had served and

apparently little disposition to create new fields of opportunity. The initial projection of strength was 2,800, the estimated number of billets in the postwar establishment that could be filled by black Marines under a policy of maintaining separate black units and the Stewards' Branch. Of this number 414 would serve at posts and stations in the U.S., 1,847 would be in ground FMF units, and 290 would serve in aviation billets. Non-available men (those sick, confined, absent, or in transit) were estimated at 249.[14]

The provision for black Marines to be a part of Marine aviation was an innovation, since none except stewards had served in air units during World War II. The Director of Aviation at Headquarters objected to the proposed assignment, indicating that he had no units which could operate separately and be composed entirely of blacks. Initially, he was overruled by the Director of the Division of Plans and Policies who rightly pointed out that the exclusion of general duty black Marines from aviation was discriminatory.[15] Nevertheless, the Director of Aviation won the argument and blacks, except stewards, were deleted from the aviation troop list by a decision of the Commandant in early June 1946.[16]

The memorandum regarding postwar employment of blacks was approved a few days earlier, on 28 May 1946. In it was a paragraph that summed up Headquarters Marine Corps' position on integration:

> It appears that the Negro question is a national issue which grows more controversial yet is more evaded as time goes by. During the past war the services were forced to bear the responsibilities of the problem, the solutions of which were often intended more to appease the Negro press and other "interested" agencies than to satisfy their own needs. It is true that a solution to the issue was, and is, to entirely eliminate any racial discriminations within the services, and to remove such practises as separate Negro units, ceilings on the number of Negroes in the respective services, etc., but it certainly appears that until the matter is settled on the higher level, the services are not required to go further than that which is already custom.[17]

While there were increasing signs that the complete integration of the services was inevitable, it was readily apparent that the leaders of the Marine Corps were not going to be in the forefront of the integration battle. Their concern was more with how they were going to utilize the black Marines they had and how they were going to recruit enough men to fill the ranks of black units.

Finding a Place

Recruiting for black Marines was suspended in the early months of 1946 until there was a clearer idea of how many veterans might become regulars and what the postwar troop requirements would be. Once the Commandant had approved the concept of employment of black Marines, Montford Point Camp again became the black boot camp. A Training Company was formed on 10 June 1946 in succession to the Recruit Training Battalion, which had been reduced to nominal strength after the last platoon had graduated in January and then been disbanded in May. Lieutenant Colonel John F. Mallard, an artilleryman who had served on Guadalcanal with the 1st Marine Division and then with the 4th Marine Division throughout the rest of the war, took command of the new company.[18] His sergeant major was Gilbert "Hashmark" Johnson, First Sergeant Edgar R. Huff became the field sergeant major, and Gunnery Sergeant Thomas Brokaw was appointed NCO in charge of recruit training. The three senior blacks all had extensive experience in recruit instruction and were determined to maintain the standards of discipline and drill with the new men which had prompted the Commanding General, Camp Lejeune, Major General John Marston, to tell a black USO audience in Jacksonville in February: "Montford Point Marines are the snappiest Marines on the entire Camp Lejeune. The others can't touch them in military discipline."[19]

As the first volunteer, Private Charles F. Boddie of Nashville, North Carolina, reported on 14 June, the last vestiges of the original boot camp area of Montford Point were disappearing. The green wooden huts that had been the home of thousands of World War II black Marines were torn down. Even Hut No. 1, which had stood at the intersection of Montford Landing Road and Harlem Drive, the receiving hut where new boots got "the word," disappeared.[20] Recruit training was now to be located in the Stewards' Branch camp, which had been built to accomodate a thousand men and now held less than a hundred.

To meet the expected influx of 1,400 volunteers who would be needed to flesh out the black Marine units, men who had been DIs before and some new instructors appeared on the drill field during the summer. The new recruits began to arrive in sufficient numbers to form four platoons and Montford Point was again ringing to the flashing cadences of the black DIs. Sergeant Major Johnson was none too happy with some of the men who were arriving, many of them enlisted for steward duty only which permitted lower mental test requirements than general duty. He did not think that they measured up to the men who had served in World War II. He commented:

> . . . the attrition rate among the recruits who came to Montford Point in 1946 and 1947 was much higher than the attrition rate of those who came in earlier, 1943 and 1944. We would start out with a platoon of 48 and if half that number completed boot camp it was a marvel. The attrition rate was outlandishly high. We seemed to be getting the scrapings of the barrel. None of the old Marines were reenlisting who had been discharged. And the only individuals left seemed to have been the 4Fs who were reclassified and we were getting them.[21]

While the new black Marines were undergoing the rigors of boot camp, there was a concerted effort on the part of Headquarters, Marine Corps to find posts and stations where they could be employed. While the barracks detachment at McAlester, Oklahoma remained a black Marine post, another Marine Barracks on the east coast was wanted. There was more than a little opposition to every posting suggested and even McAlester's days were numbered as a station for the graduates of Montford Point.

Unfortunately, the barracks at McAlester was not an ideal spot for black troops. A letter from the commanding officer, Lieutenant Colonel Clarence J. O'Donnell, of 5 November 1946, outlined some of the problems. The naval ammunition depot was located 10 miles away from McAlester which was the only available liberty area for the black Marines. Once outside the limits of the depot, the "Jim Crow" laws of Oklahoma were strictly enforced against the blacks, beginning with the bus ride into town. Once in McAlester, the men were virtually restricted to the east end of the town, an area of about three blocks. Recreation for the visiting black Marines was in competition with that of the local black population of about 2,000.

In addition to the Jim Crow laws, O'Donnell pointed out, the customs of the area brought considerable restriction and limitation. The commanding officer felt:

> . . . the Marine Corps is not now maintaining the high esteem of public opinion or gaining in prestige by the manner in which its uniform and insignia are subjected to such laws. The uniform does not count, it is relegated to the background and made to participate in and suffer the restrictions and limitations placed on it by virtue of the wearer being subject to the Jim Crow laws.[22]

It was his conclusion that for the good of the Marine Corps, black Marines should not be assigned to McAlester. In an endorsement to O'Donnell's letter, the Commanding Officer, Naval Ammunition Depot suggested that the assignment of black Marines "to areas where there is a relatively large colored population would result in the availability of far better recreation and leave areas for them."[23]

The Division of Plans and Policies received O'Donnell's letter and, after study, recommended to the Commandant that the black Marines be removed from McAlester and that the Marine Barracks, Naval Magazine, Port Chicago, California, be substituted as a post. This, combined with a plan for utilizing the Marine Barracks, Naval Ammunition Depot, Earle, New Jersey, would provide a post on each coast. The proposal was approved by General Vandegrift on 13 December 1946.[24] The Chief of Naval Operations, Fleet Admiral Chester W. Nimitz, concurred on 6 January 1947 provided the Navy's policy of non-racial discrimination was complied with.[25]

Some changes in the strength of black Marines were approved by the Commandant of 6 January 1947. The overall requirement for black personnel, which had been cut from 2,800 to 2,302, was now further reduced to 1,500. Of these, 1,150 were to be general duty Marines and 350 were to be stewards. This cut was largely due to the cancellation of requirements for antiaircraft artillery elements on Guam and Saipan, the modification of plans for utilization of the 3d AAA Battalion so as to exclude it from the planned operating forces, and a reduction in the authorized enlisted strength of the Corps by budgetary limitations.

It was decided because of the changed situation to suspend black first enlistments until 1 July 1947, at which time the subject would be restudied. The training of black recruits at Montford Point would be discontinued upon the completion of the training period of the recruits already there. Future recruit training would be conducted at the Recruit Depot, Parris Island, South Carolina, by separate black platoons, and the Stewards Schools would be moved from Montford Point to Parris Island. Second thoughts, however, brought about the revocation of the last three changes on 31 January.[26]

Plans to assign black Marines to Port Chicago received a jolt when a communication from the Commandant, 12th Naval District, dated 5 March 1947, reached Headquarters.[27] The gist of the message was that in view of present and possible future labor disturbances, it was not considered desirable to assign a black detachment to any activity in the San Francisco Bay area where labor conditions were in almost constant turmoil. The situation at Port Chicago had not improved any by 6 June, when the admiral's opinion was that "in areas predominantly white but with considerable colored population, with almost constant labor difficulties, possible clashes between colored guards and white pickets invites racial conflict."[28]

A survey in mid-1947 showed that there were approximately 2,200 black Marines out of a total Corps strength of 93,000, or about 700 more blacks than the estimated requirements. The survey indicated that those who might be considered for discharge (men with overseas service and with dependents) amounted to about the same number as the overage. The Commandant then approved certain discharges "for the convenience of the government" to reduce the number to the requirements.[29] At the same time, the requisite number of stewards was not volunteering for service nor were many men remaining in the Stewards' Branch on the expiration of enlistment. There was at least some attempt to "encourage" excess general duty black Marines to switch to steward's duty. At Headquarters, Marine Corps the action was viewed as an attempt "to solicit additional volunteers."[30] At Montford Point this translated into the word being passed to the senior black NCOs of a pending order that they would have to serve as stewards. As one of them recalled: "We were instructed that we would either sign a statement that we would serve for steward's duty only or we would accept a discharge."[31] This news, in the words of "Hashmark" Johnson, was greeted with "absolute consternation," and the majority of black general duty Marines "were determined to get out if need be rather than accept it."[32] There was vehement opposition to the proposed move, opposition that reached into influential black circles in

Washington, and the forced transfers or discharges never materialized. At Montford Point nobody signed up for steward's duty, and as one NCO recalled "we just waited to see what the hell was going to happen and it faded away." [33]

The proposed reduction in the numbers of black Marines brought about a new allocation of personnel. Port Chicago was scheduled to receive 120 men during the summer of 1947. In view of Navy opposition that had surfaced towards the assignment of blacks to Earle, New Jersey, a substitution was made of the 92-man 2d Guard Company. Marine Barracks, Naval Shipyard, Brooklyn, New York, a security detachment for the naval installations of Bayonne, New Jersey. FMF ground forces were to be two medium depot companies, one light depot company, and one depot platoon, for a total of 579 men. Training activities at Montford Point, including 180 recruits in training (60 a month), would take 337. Nonavailables would take 98, for a grand total of 1,226 general duty Marines. The removal from McAlester and the replacement of whites by blacks in the guard company at Bayonne were both to take place in July. [34]

On 18 June 1947, the plan for assignment of black Marines to Port Chicago was revoked. [35] On the same day the Commandant approached the Navy about the possibility of assigning blacks to the Marine Barracks, Naval Ammunition Depot, Hingham, Massachusetts and to the Marine Barracks, Naval Ammunition Depot, Fort Mifflin, Pennsylvania. [36] Action was deferred at the same time on the proposed assignment of black Marines to the 2d Guard Company at Bayonne. [37]

The report from Fort Mifflin indicated that the assignment of black Marines was feasible. It was suggested that a white first sergeant and four staff sergeants be retained to furnish supervision and that the replacement of certain key personnel be an overlapping procedure. Still, this was not a large detachment, as the table of organization provided for just two officers and 48 enlisted men. [38]

Numerous objections were received on the proposal to station black Marines at the Hingham ammunition depot. The commanding officer was greatly concerned with the need for skilled fire fighters and implied that black Marines might not have "the suitability or adaptability." He further pointed out that the surrounding communities were almost com-

pletely white, affording virtually no recreation, housing, or other welfare facilities. A third objection was that since this was a restricted residential area and a major summer beach resort for New England, "the assignment of Negro Marines to this command would have very adverse effect on the civilian population which would be detrimental to the Marine Corps and the Naval Service." [39]

On 10 July 1947, the Commander, Naval Base, New York, reversed the decision to send black Marines to Bayonne, and advocated their being stationed at Earle, as presenting "less problems and difficulties than at any other Naval activity." This post could utilize the services of up to 175 men. [40] A new target date of 15 August was suggested for the change from McAlester to Earle and Fort Mifflin. The Commandant approved of this but turned "thumbs down" on the initiation of active inquiry leading to the possible assignment of black troops to the Marine Barracks, Naval Operating Base, Trinidad, British West Indies. [41]

The Marine Corps hardly had time to congratulate itself on finally solving its problem when a letter came from the Chief of the Bureau of Ordnance through the Chief of Naval Operations asking for the retention of the present Marine detachment at Earle and the cancellation of orders assigning black Marines to the ammunition depot. The Navy said that a recent decision to handle ammonium nitrate at Earle had so changed the situation as to make it unwise to relieve the present trained detachment. The situation was further complicated by the introduction of contract civilian stevedores and by the planned mixing of Army MPs (white) with the Marine detachment which would involve the use of the same barracks and mess. [42]

General Vandegrift revoked the planned transfer to Earle on 20 August 1947, leaving the transfer from McAlester to Fort Mifflin unchanged. [43] Eight days later, the Division of Plans and Polices came up with the suggestion that the Marine Barracks, Naval Supply Depot, Scotia, New York, be made a black post, providing billets for 54 men. It was also planned to provide 170 additional billets by the assignment of black Marines to the Marine Barracks, Naval Ammunition Depot, Lualualei, Oahu, Hawaii. [44]

The word from Hawaii was favorable, but the Navy objected to the use of black Marines

Master Sergeant Gilbert H. "Hashmark" Johnson, sergeant major of Montford Point Camp in 1948, watches Private John W. Davis cut a stencil for a camp order. (USMC Photo 505211).

at Scotia as "weakening of the local public relations image now held by the Navy." Further objections were to the joint billeting of 25 Marine Graves Registration Escorts (white); the letter stated that the use of black Marines for Marine firing squads for the funerals of war dead would be "undesirable" and pointed out that the local black population was quite small, making for extremely limited recreational and social opportunities for black troops.[45]

The first transfer was effected on 14 September 1947 when a mass change of personnel was made at McAlester, with 112 black Marines being transferred back to Montford Point. On the same day, 50 men were sent from Montford to replace the white Marines at Fort Mifflin.

A new set of decisions was reached by the Marine Corps on 19 November 1947 when General Vandegrift approved: (1) the reopening of black enlistments at the rate of 40 a month; (2) the processing of these recruits at Montford Point; (3) the assignment of a black enlisted complement to the barracks at Earle, New Jersey, on or about 1 February 1948; and (4) the assignment a black barracks detachment to the Naval Ammunition Depot at Lualualei on or about 1 December 1948.[46]

The Navy Bureau of Ordnance again objected to the assignment of blacks to Earle, but

the Chief of Naval Operations supported the Commandant's decision with a letter concluding: "A preponderance of factors indicates no practical action other than the effectuation of the subject assignment."[47] The transfer to Earle took place on 30 January 1948 when 138 black enlisted men reported on board. A mass transfer out of white troops took place on 6 February, leaving white officers, headed by Major Bennett G. Powers. and a cadre of white NCOs. These later were later replaced by black NCOs of comparable rank.

Finally, with decisions reached as to the locations of the guard detachments, an assignment schedule for 968 general duty black Marines was drafted. Five small depot units would account for 360 men. The barracks at Earle, Fort Mifflin, and Lualualei would account for 337 men, Montford Point would take 134, with 10 in specialist schools, and 30 recruits in training, and 97 men would be non-available. The total allotted for steward's duty was 420, making the total authorized black Marine strength 1,388 men.

The Marine Corps had made an honest effort to find posts to which it could assign blacks in segregated units. The cutback in strength of the Corps overall actually advanced the cause of integration because it was becoming increasingly apparent that the maintenance of separate training facilities was uneconomical. The difficulty of finding acceptable duty stations for black units undoubtedly contributed further to the ultimate solution to the problem, the end of segregation. The final impetus was to come from the White House.

Truman and Integration

A push away from segregation in the Armed Forces and towards integration was furnished by the organization on 23 November 1947 of the Committee Against Jim Crow in Military Service and Training. The two most prominent leaders were A. Philip Randolph, president of the Brotherhood of Sleeping Car Porters, and Grant Reynolds, formerly a Republican city councilman from Harlem. Headquarters for the new committee was the New York union office of the Sleeping Car Porters. The basic principle implied in the organization's title received strong support from black citizens and the black press.[48]

The climate was right to provide effective political pressure against segregation because

President Harry Truman, on the recommendation of the Joint Chiefs of Staff, was ready to propose the imposition of a peacetime draft. On 17 March 1948, he asked Congress to enact such legislation. Just five days later, Mr. Randolph led a delegation to the White House where he reportedly told the President that blacks did not want "to shoulder a gun to fight for democracy abroad unless they get democracy at home." [49]

When the public portions of the hearings on the draft bill were reached, Mr. Randolph challenged the Senate Armed Services Committee with his statement: "Today I would like to make it clear to this committee and through you to Congress and the American people that passage now of a Jim Crow draft may only result in mass civil disobedience." [50] Although it was approved by many blacks, the Randolph declaration did not go unchallenged. At Montford Point, now-titled Master Sergeant "Hashmark" Johnson wrote a long letter to President Truman on 31 March taking exception to Mr. Randolph's extreme position, calling it "biased and dangerous." He assured the President "that whatever crisis comes, foreign or domestic, the American Negro will be in there pitching for all he is worth, alongside other fellow Americans." His letter, forwarded through channels, reached the President who replied that he had read it "with a great deal of interest." [51]

Sergeant Johnson had not been demoted. His new rank was the result of a sweeping change of designations. On 1 December 1946, the Marine Corps had done away with the multiplicity of enlisted rank titles that had grown up during the war and the years before and settled on one title for each of the seven enlisted pay grades: Master Sergeant; Technical Sergeant; Staff Sergeant; Sergeant; Corporal; Private First Class; and Private. Sergeant Major Johnson, for example, became a master sergeant but still retained the appointment of sergeant major.

When the new peacetime draft act was signed into law on 24 June 1948, President Truman was not long in following it with an anti-discrimination order. After the Democratic National Convention in July which featured a dramatic walkout of southern delegates following a losing battle over a liberal civil rights plank, the President promulgated Executive Order 9981 on 26 July 1948 which banned color bias in the Armed Services. A

seven man board to be named later, and titled "President's Committee on Equality of Treatment and Opportunity in the Armed Services," was to investigate rules and practises to see if changes should be made. Mr. Truman assured reporters on 29 July that racial segregation would eventually be abolished in all services. [52]

The President announced the membership of his committee on 18 September 1948. Best known as the "Fahy Committee" after its chairman, former U.S. Solicitor General Charles H. Fahy, it included A. J. Donahue, Dwight R. G. Palmer, Charles Luckman, William E. Stevenson, Lester Granger, and John A. Sengstacke as members. [53] The committee conducted its inquiries with a spirit of understanding and cooperation with the Armed Services, but still it prodded and prompted more effective compliance with existing regulations which if conscientiously carried out would have ended segregation in time. A particular target was all-black units and the philosophy that kept them in being. When the committee made its report to the President in 1950 just prior to the outbreak of the Korean War, *Time* magazine commented on its findings:

> The committee did not argue the moral or sociological aspects of the case. It based its arguments on efficiency. There were bright Negroes and there were dumb ones, just like white men. To refuse a job to an intelligent or skilled Negro was simply a waste of manpower. Concentration of unskilled Negroes in segregated units just multiplied their inefficiency. [54]

Some officers at Marine Corps Headquarters felt rather strongly that it was not the Marine Corps place to lead the fight against segregation. On 17 March 1949, the Commandant, General Clifton D. Cates, objected to a proposed directive of the Armed Forces Personnel Policy Board, another civilian review panel, which advocated a policy of equality of treatment and opportunity for all persons in the Armed Forces without regard to race, color, religion, or national origin.

General Cates first indicated that he thought the board had exceeded its authority in developing the draft directive. It was his feeling that the National Military Establishment could not "be an agency for experimentation in civil liberty without detriment to its ability to maintain the efficiency and high state of readiness so essential to national defense." The Commandant supported the principle that "allocation of personnel on a qualitative and quantitative basis to meet the needs of the Armed

Forces should be made without regard to race, color, religion or national origin," but protested vigorously that:

> The problem of segregation is not the responsibility of the Armed Forces but is a problem of the nation. Changing national policy in this respect through the Armed Forces is a dangerous path to pursue in as much as it affects the ability of the National Military Establishment to fulfill its mission . . . Should the time arise that non-segregation, and this term applies to white as well as negro, is accepted as a custom of the nation, this policy can be adopted without detriment by the National Military Establishment." [51]

Like General Holcomb's remarks in 1942 before blacks entered the Marine Corps. General Cates' opinions had little effect upon the course of change. On 20 April 1949, Secretary of Defense Louis Johnson ordered the Armed Services to end racial discrimination in line with President Truman's Executive Order 9981. The Secretary's directive provided that "all individuals, regardless of race, will be accorded equal opportunity for appointment, advancement, professional improvement, promotion." Segregated units could continue but on a permissive rather than a mandatory basis. [56]

Secretary of the Navy Francis P. Matthews issued ALNAV 49–447 on 23 June 1949 which was a landmark declaration of racial policy in the Navy and the Marine Corps, dealing as it did with racial segregation as well as discrimination. The pertinent portions read:

> 2. It is the policy of the Navy Department that there shall be equality of treatment and opportunity for all persons in the Navy and Marine Corps without regard to race, color, religion, or national origin.
> 3. In their attitude and day-to-day conduct of affairs, officers and enlisted personnel of the Navy and Marine Corps shall adhere rigidly and impartially to the Navy Regulations, in which no distinction is made between individuals wearing the uniform of these services.
> 4. All personnel will be enlisted or appointed, trained, advanced or promoted, assigned duty, and administered in all respects without regard to race, color, religion, or national origin.
> 5. In the utilization of housing, messing, berthing, and other facilities, no special or unusual provisions will be made for the accomodation of any minority race. [57]

A few months later, on 18 November 1949, the Marine Corps issued a memorandum of guidance to commanders establishing policy regarding black Marines. It revoked all previous policy statements including those prohibiting mixed units. However, all black units of platoon strength or larger, both regular and reserve, were to be continued. Commanders of organized reserve units could accept or reject men for their unit, but not on the basis of race, color, religion, or national origin. Most important (and this appears to be the official beginning of integration in the Marine Corps), it stated: "Individual negro Marines will be assigned in accordance with MOS [Military Occupational Specialty] to vacancies in any unit where their services can be effectively utilized." [58]

The memorandum actually postdated the end of Montford Point as a segregated facility and the dispersal of its men to both mixed and black units. In practice, the process of desegregation had begun in the Marine Corps on a gradual, local, and ad hoc basis well before the official word filtered down.

The End In Sight

Athletic teams, in the Marine Corps as in civilian life, were one of the first means of integration in the postwar period. At Camp Lejeune black all stars from the Montford Point teams which played in camp intra-unit competition were selected to play on camp teams which engaged in inter-service play. In the 1947–1948 season, the Montford Point basketball team won the intra-unit competition and some of its star members became part of the team that represented Camp Lejeune. In other sports, the athletic abilities of some black Marines won them a place on other camp teams, particularly in track, football, and boxing. Boxing had been an integrated sport overseas during the war and it continued to be one after the fighting ended; it was foolish to deny men a place on the team on the basis of race when Montford Point harbored men like Sergeant Charles W. Riggs, formerly of the 35th Marine Depot Company, who had been the All Service Heavyweight Champion of Pacific Ocean Areas, Forward, on Guam. [59]

Although black Marines continued to be quartered on a segregated basis, increasing numbers of blacks began to work side by side with whites on the basis of common military occupational specialities. Letter of Instruction 421 of 20 March 1943, which had directed that no black Marines would be placed in positions where they would command whites, was rescinded on 14 February 1946. [60] As the natural course of events evolved, situations arose where black NCOs of necessity were placed in the position where they were responsible for giving orders to white Marines junior to them. Such events were not commonplace but they did occur, and it was prejudicial to discipline to allow any exception to the general rules of military precedence and order.

The number of black Marines was so relatively small that it became uneconomical in the austere postwar period to continue separate training facilities for specialists at Montford Point. Stewards, cooks, bakers, and eventually all specialists were trained at Camp Lejeune schools, in mixed classes for the most part. The necessary recruit influx to maintain the number of blacks authorized on active duty was small and recruit training was switched to Parris Island in the spring of 1949 as a measre of efficiency and economy. At first there were separate black platoons under black DIs, but by fall the decision was made to effect complete integration.

The Commanding General, Marine Corps Recruit Depot, Parris Island, during this period was Major General Alfred H. Noble, who recalled in an oral history interview:

> Also while I was there we integrated for the first time the black people into the Marine Corps recruit platoons right with the white trainees. This was done as soon as they arrived at Parris Island. I believe I said some time ago that before that time we would wait for the number of colored troops to build up to the proper size of a recruit platoon and then they trained as a separate unit. While I was there the NCO clubs also were opened up to the colored non-commissioned officers. This innovation not only produced no unfavorable reaction among the Marines, but it also had no unfavorable reaction among the civilian citizens of South Carolina in the vicinity. Of course, I consulted the civilian leaders first and told them what I was going to do and got their advice and promises of help to try and stop any adverse criticism of it. It seemed like integration was due to take place sooner or later anyway in this country, certainly in the Armed Forces, and I thought that it should take place in the Armed Forces first.[61]

General Noble's remarks indicate that the opposition to integration in the Marine Corps was by no means universal at the highest levels. Many Marines, white and black, shared his views that the Armed Forces were in a unique position to promote desegregation. But there were plenty of white Marines of all ranks who preferred the racial *status quo* and the treatment by some of these men of the first black regular officer was described by him as "unsympathetic."[62]

John E. Rudder, born in Paducah, Kentucky, served in the 51st Defense Battalion after his enlistment in June 1943 and was selected for the V-12 program, attending Purdue University. After his discharge in 1946, he continued at Purdue as a regular NROTC (Naval Reserve Officer Training Corps) midshipman destined for a regular commission. In June 1948, he was appointed a second lieutenant, USMC, and in September started the Basic School course for new officers. Upon reconsideration of his circumstances, Lieutenant Rudder decided to resign his commission, stating to a black reporter that his reason "could be described as religious scruples."[63] He was honorably discharged on 1 April 1949.

At the same time Rudder was appointed, June 1948, William K. Jenkins from Elizebeth, New Jersey, a contract NROTC graduate from Illinois Polytechnic Institute and a Navy veteran of World War II, was commissioned a reserve second lieutenant and assigned to inactive duty. Lieutenant Jenkins, in 1973 a reserve lieutenant colonel, was called to active duty in the Korean War, where he became the first black officer to lead Marines in combat as both a weapons and a rifle platoon commander with Company B, 1st Battalion, 7th Marines.

Another segregation barrier was broken in 1949 when the first black women enlisted in the Marine Corps. During World War II, the lack of separate housing facilities, plus the fact that white Women Reserves early filled the authorized complement for women acted against blacks being enlisted. On the passage of the Women's Armed Services Integration Act of 12 June 1948, women became a part of the regular Marine Corps for the first time.[64] In November, the first officers and enlisted women, all veterans of World War II service, were sworn in as regulars and provisions were made for limited recruiting. On 8 March 1949, Mr. A. Philip Randolph, acting for the Committee Against Jim Crow, directed a question to the Commandant: "We should like to ascertain if Negro women were eligible to join the Marines and if so whether on a basis of non-segregation."[65] General Cates' reply two days later said: "If qualified for enlistment, negro women will be accepted on the same basis as other applicants."[66]

Six months later on 8 September 1949 the first black woman Marine, Annie E. Graham, enlisted at Detroit, Michigan, and on the following day Ann E. Lamb joined at New York

Warrant Officer Annie L. Grimes, the third black woman to enlist in the Marine Corps in 1950, is shown in 1968 with Colonel Barbara J. Bishop, Director of Women Marines. (USMC Photo 4416512).

City. The two women reported to Parris Island on 10 September and went through boot camp together with Platoon 5-A of the 3d Recruit Training Battalion. Both subsequently reported for duty at Headquarters Marine Corps. The third black woman to join, Annie L. Grimes of Chicago, who was destined to become a chief warrant officer later in her career, joined and went to boot camp in February 1950. From the beginning, the reception, training, and housing of black women Marines was completely integrated.

The treatment accorded black women was undoubtedly a reflection of what was happening elsewhere in the Corps. Not all black general duty Marines in 1949 were being assigned to segregated units, scattered individuals began to show up on the rolls of previously all-white commands in accordance with their MOSs. But the real turning point away from segregated units awaited the closing of

Montford Point Camp as a black training center and barracks area.

The strength of the troops in the camp remained about the same during 1949, roughly six officers and 300 enlisted men. Major Frank W. Ferguson, by then the camp commander, also doubled in brass as the supply officer. Ferguson, a former quartermaster clerk who had fought and been captured at Corregidor, had served at Montford Point since March 1946 and was destined to preside over the dissolution of the segregated facility.[67] On 9 September 1949, Headquarters Company, Montford Point Camp was deactivated and the remaining 242 officers and men on the rolls were transferred, for the most part to other Camp Lejeune units.

The deactivation marked the end of an era for black Marines; it came just a little over seven years after the first boots had reported for training. To some black Marines it meant the end of an ordered and familiar existence where they were sure of coming "home" to Montford Point periodically. One veteran, Edgar R. Huff, then a master sergeant, expressed this view when he commented on the effect of the official advent of integration, recalling:

> . . . that was a sad day, it was a black day, a black mark as far as I'm concerned. Myself, and to my knowledge the majority of black Marines . . . we wanted to stay together, we had our own camp, we had our own resources, and we were taken care of, holding our own we called it at that time, and didn't care to go anyplace. I was sorry to see it happen.[68]

From a somewhat different point of view, "Hashmark" Johnson, who at the time Montford Point closed down was sergeant major of the barracks at Earle, New Jersey, commented on the attitude of the black Marines towards integration:

> Some of them saw it as a gradual phasing out of the Negro Marine and others saw it as an opportunity to show they were equal in proficiency and all other qualifications to their white counterparts. Some welcomed the opportunity and others were just a bit scared of it.[69]

Scared, pleased, unhappy, or indifferent, black Marines had at last achieved a goal that many people both inside and outside the Marine Corps had worked for. There were still all-black units in the Corps, but there were integrated units as well, and the trend was irreversibly towards a completely integrated Marine Corps. The outbreak of the Korean War measurably accelerated the desegregation process.

CHAPTER 6

A DECADE OF INTEGRATION

On 30 June 1950, immediately following the outbreak of the Korean War, there were 1,502 black Marines on active duty, 1,075 on general duty assignments and 427 serving as stewards.[1] In overall strength the Marine Corps stood at 74,279, its post-World War II low.[2] Three years later, as the war was drawing to a close, 14,731 black Marines were on active duty, only 538 of whom were stewards. The overall strength of the Marine Corps was 249,219, its peak for the Korean War.[3] The growth in the number of black Marines from two percent of the Corp's strength to six percent accurately reflected the end of segregation. Certainly the manpower demands of the war hastened the change, but the combat performance of black Marines in integrated units did nothing to lessen the pace.

In July 1950, a thin sprinkling of blacks went out to Korea with the first units to see combat in the Pusan Perimeter, the 1st Provisional Marine Brigade, which included the 5th Marines and Marine Aircraft Group 33. Still more men followed in August and September when the 1st Marine Division and the 1st Marine Aircraft Wing deployed to take part in the amphibious assault at Inchon and the capture of Seoul. Men from barracks detachments, including those at Earle, Ft. Mifflin, and Lualualei, from 2d Marine Division units, and from virtually every post and station in the Marine Corps were used to bring the deployed units up to war strength. Typically, the 6th Marines of the 2d Division, augmented by recalled reservists and men from the supporting establishment, was used as a nucleus to form the 7th Marines of the 1st Division. The regimental commander, Colonel Homer A. Litzenberg, Jr., recalled, after his men had fought their way out of the Chosin Reservoir trap, that "one of the miscellaneous units he received" when he activated the 7th Marines "was a 54-man Negro service unit which was integrated throughout the command." He commented to the press:

> Never once did any color problem bother us . . . . It just wasn't any problem. We had one Negro sergeant in command of an all-white squad and there was another—with a graves registration unit—who was one of the finest Marines I've ever seen.[4]

These remarks coming from one of the Corps distinguished combat leaders, a highly decorated former enlisted man with nearly 30 years of active service,[5] were echoed by the division commander, then Major General Oliver P. Smith. In an oral history memoir of his career, the general was asked if his division was integrated. He replied:

> Oh yes, I had a thousand Negroes, and we had no racial troubles. The men did whatever they were qualified to do. There were communicators, there were cooks, there were truck drivers, there were plain infantry—they did everything, and they did a good job because they were integrated, and they were with good people . . . . Two of these Negroes got the Navy Cross. There was no fooling; they were real citations, and there were plenty of Silvers Stars and Bronze Stars, and what have you. And I had no complaint on their performance of duty.[6]

The mention of the Navy Cross awards highlights a peculiar problem that arises when the story of black Marines in the Korean War is researched. Short of the lengthy task of matching up the individual record books of every recipient of a medal with his citation, there is no way of determining which of these men was black. Records pertaining to black Marines, aside from strength and deployment statistics, are virtually nonexistent. With the end of segregation, black Marines merged into the mainstream of Marine Corps experience.

Throughout much of the Korean War and the decade that followed, the trace of black Marines is extremely hard to follow. There are no pertinent unit records for there were no black units. Moreover, there was a conscious policy of cutting down on the number and variety of reports which included race as a reporting element. In June of 1953, there were 30 such records required by various Depart-

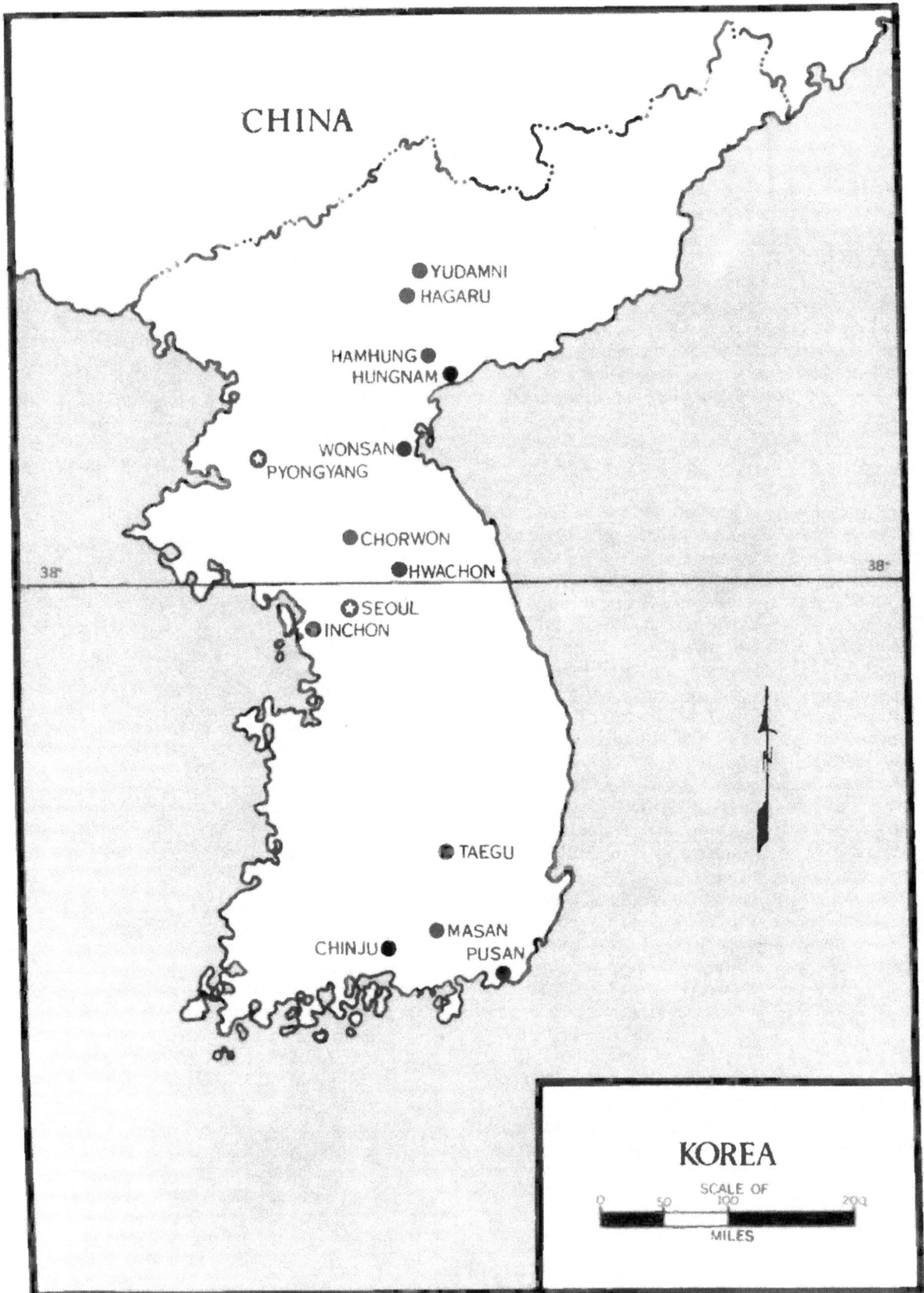

CHINA

●YUDAMNI
●HAGARU

HAMHUNG●
HUNGNAM●

WONSAN●●
PYONGYANG✪

●CHORWON
●HWACHON

38°   38°

✪SEOUL
●INCHON

●TAEGU

●MASAN
CHINJU● PUSAN

KOREA

SCALE OF

0   50   100   200

MILES

ment of Defense agencies; 17 of these were eliminated. By April 1954 the number of records with a racial reporting element was down to 10. Many of these few were required only to ensure that personnel assignments were equitably made.[7] In large part, therefore, the narrative thread of the story of black Marines in the 1950s has been extracted from the experiences and reminiscences of a few representative officers and men whose careers spanned these years. Fortunately, they were perceptive observers as well as being intimately a part of the process of change.

Combat In Korea

Among the various scattered records of black Marines there is an occasional human interest story that highlights the advent of integration. On 5 December 1949, a black World War II veteran, former Corporal Walter Chandler, wrote to Headquarters Marine Corps from his home in Addyston, Ohio asking if the Marine Corps' recruiting advertisements broadcast over the radio were meant for whites only or for any Americans able and willing to serve. If blacks were being accepted, he wanted to recommend a young man by the name of Donald Woody as a potential Marine. In reply, Headquarters asked Mr. Woody to contact the local recruiter in Cincinnati, Ohio; if found qualified he would be welcome.[8] The sequel is found in the casualty files of Headquarters where it is noted the Corporal Donald Woody served with Company I, 3d Battalion, 7th Marines in Korea and was wounded twice in combat.[9]

Thousands of black Marines matched Corporal Woody's experience in fighting side-by-side with white Marines as part of the same unit. They were needed and they were accepted for what they were. As one young white lieutenant, Herbert M. Hart, wrote to his college newspaper in late 1952 regarding his battalion:

> It doesn't make any difference if you are white, red, black, green, or turquoise to the men over here. No record is kept by color. When we receive a draft of men they are assigned by name and experience only . . . There's no way we can find out a man's color until we see him and by that time he's already in a foxhole, an integral part of his team.[10]

As one of Hart's men commented: "After you've been here a while, you'll see that color doesn't make any difference. It's the guts that

Having fired his 57mm recoilless rifle at Chinese Communist positions, a black Marine gunner heads for cover in case of incoming enemy fire. (USMC Photo A173312).

count." And as the lieutenant observed, "color doesn't seem to be any register of guts."[11]

Certainly he had ample evidence of this in his own unit. PFC (later Corporal) A C Clark, a short-statured black automatic riflemen from Minden, Louisiana serving with Company H, 3d Battalion, 5th Marines, won a Silver Star on 13 December 1952 for aggressively covering the evacuation of two wounded Marines of his combat patrol, silencing an enemy machine gun, killing three enemy soldiers, and helping to evacuate other American casualties although wounded twice himself.[12] Since PFC Clark previously had been awarded a Bronze Star for rescuing his wounded platoon leader on another combat patrol in August, he "served" as one of his citations states "to inspire all who observed him."[13]

There were other black Marines like Clark, recognized combat heroes, and there were legions of those who did their jobs in an unspectacular, steady, and efficient manner. The continual flow of replacements soon brought some of the senior black line NCOs to Korea, men who had been leaders in segregated units and who now took their place in previously all-white units. Master Sergeant Edgar R. Huff, who had been the guard chief of the Marine Barracks at Earle, ended up as gunnery sergeant of Weapons Company, 2d Battalion, 1st Marines. Moving into the infantry replacement training cycle at Camp Pendleton in June 1951, he was platoon commander of a "Zebra" platoon, composed entirely of white staff NCOs, and noted that he "certainly couldn't have been treated any better than I was" in his first experience in an integrated outfit.[14] When he arrived at his battalion's lines on the east central front in Korea, he found himself the only black man in his company and an object of some awe and speculation as he stood about six foot, five inches tall and was built along the lines of a professional football lineman. In his words:

> I decided the first thing for me to do was to call my company together and let them see this monster that they had been hearing about . . . . [I told them] that I was the company gunnery sergeant, and I wanted them to know that under all circumstances I was the company gunnery sergeant, not the figurehead, but the company gunnery sergeant, and they understood that . . . . [15]

Huff's experience of being the only black Marine in a company-sized unit was not uncommon in 1950 and 1951, but it became far less so as the war continued. Over 10,000 blacks joined the Corps between June 1951 and July 1952 and many of these men reached Korea to serve in combat.[16] Scattered throughout the 1st Division and 1st Wing, they filled the billets for which their training and experience fitted them, and they earned the respect of their fellow Marines in direct ratio to how well they did their job. When a veteran NCO like Master Sergeant Gilbert "Hashmark" Johnson arrived in Korea, he was given a progression of responsible jobs which fitted his background: personnel chief of the 1st Shore Party Battalion; first sergeant of the battalion's Company A; personnel sergeant major of the forward echelon of the 2d Battalion, 1st Marines; and administrative advisor at the Headquarters of the Korean Marine Corps. Asked if he had experienced any problems as a senior black NCO serving in predominantly white units, Johnson characteristically said: "I didn't encounter any difficulty. I accepted each individual for what he was and apparently they accepted me for what I was."[17]

Led by a black Marine, a light machine gun squad of Company D, 3d Battalion, 1st Marines moves up to reinforce the front lines in July 1953. (USMC Photo A173715).

Black Leaders

While there were thousands of black enlisted men who served in Korea, there was only a handful of black officers. Lieutenant William K. Jenkins, the first black officer to lead Marines in combat, served as platoon leader with Company B, 1st Battalion, 7th Marines in 1951–1952. A few other ground officers reached Korea during the fighting and one pilot, Second Lieutenant Frank E. Petersen, Jr.

The first black officer to be commissioned in the Marine Corps from the Naval Aviation Cadet Program, Petersen was only the fourth of his race to receive the naval aviator designation. In choosing an aviation career, he was particularly inspired by the example of Ensign Jesse L. Brown, the first black naval aviator, who was killed while flying close support for the Marines breaking out from the Chosin Reservoir on 4 December 1950. Petersen, from Topeka, Kansas, enlisted in the Navy after a year of college and then entered the cadet program. Determined to be the first black Marine pilot, he received both his wings and his commission at Pensacola on 1 October 1952. After advanced flight training in the States, he reported to Marine Attack Squadron 212 in Korea in April 1953. Flying the attack version Corsair, Petersen completed 64 combat missions before the fighting ended, earning a Distinguished Flying Cross and six Air Medals. In 1973 he was the senior black regular officer in the Marine Corps as a lieutenant colonel.[18]

Most of the black officers who were commissioned during the war were reserves who were released to inactive duty after completing a normal tour, but a few like Petersen stayed on to become regulars. Kenneth H. Berthoud, Jr. from New York City, the second officer to receive a regular commission, was a graduate of Long Island University with a major in biology. A naval reserve hospital corpsman while attending school, he entered the Marine Corps as a candidate for a commission and was designated a second lieutenant in the reserve on 13 December 1952 and a regular officer on 13 July 1953. Posted overseas to serve as a tank officer in the 3d Marine Division in Japan, he also served with the 1st Tank Battalion on occupation duty in Korea. Subsequently becoming a supply officer, he served in many responsible assignments in the logistics field and in 1973 was a lieutenant colonel assigned to Headquarters Marine Corps in the Installations and Logistics Department.[19]

Another black officer, Hurdle L. Maxwell, enlisted in the Marine Corps during the Korean War after three years at Indiana State Teachers College and was commissioned a reserve second lieutenant in March 1953 and a regular officer in September after completing The Basic School at Quantico. Like Kenneth Berthoud, he served originally as a tank officer with the 3d and 1st Tank Battalions in Japan and Korea; he later held other staff and command assignments in FMF and supporting establishment units. In January 1969, three months after his promotion to lieutenant colonel, he reported to the 2d Marine Division to become the first black officer to command an infantry battalion, the 1st Battalion, 6th Marines. Lieutenant Colonel Maxwell retired in 1971 after serving on active duty for over 20 years.[20]

These few men, and others who slowly followed them into the Marine Corps to serve as pilots and ground officers in the 1950s, had to have, of necessity, a special quality of personal integrity and professional pride. They could never be inconspicuous wherever they served; they were, in a real sense, marked men. They represented black Marines as a group and whatever they did, however well they performed their jobs, was to many men the

First black Marine pilot, Second Lieutenant Frank E. Petersen, Jr., climbs into his Corsair shortly after arriving in Korea in April 1953. (USMC Photo A347177).

measure of what could be expected from black Marines in leadership positions. Never until the Vietnam era more than a small fraction of one percent of active duty officers, the black officers were well aware of their role and their responsibilities. There were few situations where they could afford to relax and none where they could afford to be average officers.

While all black officers in the 1950s were relatively junior in rank, there were a number of blacks in the top enlisted pay grade, master sergeant, men who had comparable time in the Corps with their white contemporaries. As they had in integrated units in combat in Korea, these black NCOs began to fill more and more leadership positions in peacetime units. One of these men was Edgar R. Huff, who was to establish an unbeatable string of firsts for black Marines, each one noted with pride by his fellow blacks who thereafter followed him into comparable positions.

In September 1952, shortly after he returned from Korea, Huff became the gunnery sergeant and then the first sergeant of Weapons Company, 2d Battalion, 8th Marines at Camp Lejeune. In February 1954, he became the battalion sergeant major, the first black to hold such a position in an infantry battalion. In April 1955, he reported to the Marine Barracks, Port Lyautey, Morocco to serve as guard chief. At the end of the year he became the barracks sergeant major with the rank of sergeant major.

The Marine Corps had determined in 1955 to reinstitute the actual ranks of first sergeant and sergeant major within the top pay grade. Selection boards sat at Headquarters Marine Corps to pick the men who would hold both ranks from the master sergeants with combat and combat support occupational specialties. Huff was the only black Marine among those selected to both first sergeant and sergeant major. On 31 December 1955, he became a sergeant major, a rank he was to hold on active duty for almost 17 years until he was the senior sergeant major in point of service in the Marine Corps. As a revealing side light to Huff's promotion, the white master sergeant who had been sergeant major at Port Lyautey and who had not been selected for the higher rank indicated that he would rather retire than serve under a black man. The commanding officer of the barracks immediately contacted Headquarters Marine Corps, which adjudged the master sergeant's usefulness to the Marine Corps had ended and retired him as soon as he could be returned to the United States.[21] Both the promotion and the retirement were a far cry from the days of segregation.

Huff went on in later assignments in the 1950s and early 1960s to become regimental sergeant major of the 2d Force Service Regiment at Camp Lejeune (1957–59), command sergeant major of Landing Force Training Command, Atlantic in Norfolk (1959–60), and regimental sergeant major of 3d Force Service Regiment on Okinawa (1961–62). His path to advancement was not always smooth and the cooperation received from some white officers and NCOs was not always exemplary for the first black sergeant major in every post he occupied. He was to recall later regarding his initial service in the 2d Force Service Regiment that "I did everything, bit my tongue till it scarred the bottom of my stomach, to get along with these people and also maintain the dignity of the position I held . . . And it was very difficult for me to do this."[22] But he had the whole-hearted support of his commanding officer, Colonel Harlan C. Cooper, a Naval Academy graduate (Class of 1931) who had commanded the 1st Base Depot and the 16th

Field Depot during World War II.[23] Cooper soon made it evident to all concerned that Sergeant Major Huff was the regimental sergeant major and spoke with the colonel's authority in all matters concerning the enlisted men of the regiment.

There were many white commanding officers and senior NCOs like Colonel Cooper, men who were determined to make integration work. It was the official Marine Corps policy, often expressed in some variation of the catch phrase "every Marine is a green Marine." If, in retrospect, this attitude seems an oversimplification of a very complex problem, it was a pervading philosophy at the time. Although some white Marines harbored personal reservations and prejudices about integration, and others indulged in foot-dragging and showed thinly-masked hostility toward the effort, the main thrust of most Marines was toward the official goal.

In a sense, while Sergeant Major Huff led the way in many responsible senior enlisted assignments, his experiences were shared by other regular black line NCOs. They too had their chances to fill important billets that required judgement, maturity, and leadership. During most of the years following the Korean war, the number of black Marines stayed around 12–13,000 men and women while the enlisted strength of the Corps overall fluctuated from 205,275 (1954) to a low of 154,242 (1960).[24] Although the number of blacks remained below 10 percent, the ratio was substantially higher than it had been in the pre-Korea years. Many of these Marines had served since World War II and risen to the top pay grades. They were routinely assigned to the positions to which their rank and seniority entitled them. It became common for both black and white Marines to have blacks as their senior NCOs. The measure of a Marine was slowly but surely becoming how well he did his job, not what color his skin was.

Changing Times

Within the Marine Corps, the last vestige of military segregation at the end of the Korean War lay in the Stewards' Branch. The black Marines assigned to stewards' duty were still recruited under Steward Duty Only enlistment contracts or were augmented by volunteers from general duty blacks. There was a strong feeling among many of the stewards that this volunteering was rigged and that men were assigned, presumably whenever the need arose, by manipulating their general classification test scores. Investigation showed there was at least some support for the truth of this rumor in local instances.[25] For many young blacks, there was a stigma attached to being an officers' steward; some obviously felt their position was subject to ridicule, particularly by other blacks. They did not like the thought of being irrevocably confined to one specialty, a specialty that was itself limited to blacks.

Two senior black steward NCOs, Technical Sergeants James E. Johnson and Leo McDowell, had both made a number of sugges-

tions to higher headquarters during the early 50s regarding the improvement of the quality of mess service and the quality of service life for stewards. In the spring of 1953, the Quartermaster General of the Marine Corps, Major General W. P. T. Hill, called the two men to Headquarters Marine Corps to listen to what they had to say. He gave them a chance to act on their recommendations and appointed them members of a Steward Inspection and Demonstration Team, later joined by white Warrant Officer Perry S. Brenton, which began to tour east and west coast officers' messes after developing a syllabus at Camp Lejeune. Aside from teaching advanced

Vice Chairman of the Civil Service Commission, the Honorable James E. Johnson, a retired Marine chief warrant officer (middle), sits with General Lewis W. Walt, Assistant Commandant of the Marine Corps, and Mr. Richard L. Dalton, President of the Montford Point Marine Association, at a parade in Mr. Johnson's honor at the Marine Barracks, Washington in 1969. (USMC Photo A419277).

techniques of mess cooking, service, and management, the two blacks inquired deeply into the living conditions and motivations of the men with whom they talked. They found that many stewards were dissatisfied with what they considered overly-long working hours, limited chances for advancement and in-service education, and, particularly, with the image of the Stewards' Branch as a place where they were "condemned" to serve as long as they were Marines.

Both Johnson and McDowell emphasized the positive side of stewards' duty, the chance of learning a trade that was a salable commodity in civilian life. They pointed out that stewards often had the opportunity to improve on their service pay. As Johnson noted:

> . . . those young men who were stewards were able to make extra money because they had the skills. They were good bartenders and they always made extra money. They were good waiters and they could go to any restaurant and they made money. They were good caterers; they made extra money when they went out.[26]

Setting an example of their own, both NCOs were heavily involved in off-duty educational courses and encouraged the black stewards to do the same after making sure through their efforts that adequate time was available to the men for this purpose.

Johnson, a most unusual man with a tremendous reservoir of talents, was also to show that it was really possible to advance as a result of doing a steward's job in a superior fashion. He was appointed a warrant officer in 1960 in the food administration field. He went on to hold supply and administrative billets, continuing all the while to increase his educational background. Shortly after he retired as a chief warrant officer in July 1965, he received his bachelor of arts degree, later to be joined by a degree of master of arts; he then went on to work for both juris doctor and doctor of philosophy degrees. In civilian life, he became in turn a very successful insurance salesman, the California State Commissioner of Veterans Affairs, the Vice Chairman of the Federal Civil Service Commission, and the Assistant Secretary of the Navy for Manpower and Reserve Affairs. All this was accomplished in the space of eight years by a man who had entered a segregated Marine Corps in 1944 as a private with a record book stamped "Colored" and an enlistment contract "Steward Duty Only."

Among the recommendations forwarded to General Hill by the Brenton-Johnson-McDowell team was one that emerged in a favorable climate in 1954—to eliminate Steward Duty Only enlistments. The Secretary of the Navy did this for both the Navy and the Marine Corps on 1 March 1954.[27] The team also felt strongly that men who wanted to get out of the Stewards' Branch into other fields in the Marine Corps should have the opportunity to do so. When this came to pass, despite dire predictions of a wholesale exodus of black stewards, only 5-10 percent of the men opted for transfer. The ultimate step was to integrate the steward service field and this began to happen while Major General Joseph C. Burger commanded Camp Lejeune in 1956–57.[28] As white stewards increased in number the very human reaction of some black stewards was to try to hang on to choice jobs that they had. For now these positions were viewed in a different light. As then Warrant Officer Johnson later observed about the black stewards:

> . . . they felt they were being discriminated against because they were all black. That was the real hang-up, you see. But the moment they opened it [stewards' duty], they said, "O. K., fine. It's all right." Because their feeling was that if it was so good, why don't you have some of the whites in it.[29]

The gradual change in the image of stewards' duty and the attitude toward it by both black and white Marines was in a way a reflection of the immense social revolution that had its start in the 1950s. Like the integration of the Stewards' Branch, the racial integration of many other aspects of American life came about both as the result of evolutional change and governmental intervention. Within the Marine Corps, there was no question that official policy called for the end of segregation, but the off-duty actions and attitudes of many white Marines belied this. These men were the products of home backgrounds where legal or *de facto* segregation was a way of life and they either approved of or went along with local customs and laws which demanded segregation in schools, housing, public places, and transportation facilities.

An inequitable situation existed in which black and white Marines served side by side in the ranks, but their children were separated in schools both on post and off. Off-base housing was often segregated and military quarters areas tended to be segregated too, movie theaters, even some on base, had separate racial seating areas, and commercial buses serving military posts in the South required blacks to sit in the rear. A black officer or enlisted man in Jacksonville, North Carolina, for instance, could be and was barred from normal civilian activities which were open to any of their white counterparts. This was an unhealthy situation, one which would take many years to change, but such change was indeed coming.

In a monumental decision that had far-ranging repercussions, the Supreme Court ruled on 17 May 1954 that racial segregation in public schools was unconstitutional. The decision noted that: "Separate educational facilities are inherently unequal." [30] Even before this ruling was published, the Secretary of Defense, Charles E. Wilson, had ordered the Armed Forces to end school desegregation on military posts by 1 September 1955. [31] If necessary, the Federal Government would operate the schools if local school districts did not comply with the order.

Subsequent rulings by the Supreme Court in cases which challenged the "separate but equal" doctrine, which had the force of law in the South and of custom in many other areas of the country, barred segregation in public recreational facilities (1955) and on board public transport vehicles (1956). [32] Civil rights bills were passed by the Congress in 1957 and 1960 which were intended to ensure blacks a right to vote and to set up enforcement means that would guarantee unfettered elections. [33]

There was vehement and all too often violent opposition to the end of legal segregation in many parts of the country. No amount of legislation or court rulings or government edicts could change long-held racial biases overnight. The pace of integration was often halting in the decade following the Korean War as legal challenges and illegal subterfuges were combined by white leaders to slow proceedings. Many American blacks, tired of "second-class citizen" status, were understandably impatient to experience the substance of meaningful integration. Black leaders could suddenly count on newly awakened racial awareness and solidarity, and at times militancy, to back their demands for civil rights progress. The rising generation of young black men and women was determined to live in an environment more to their own choosing than had been the lot of their parents.

This new consciousness of black individual and collective rights and worth would lead to many challenges to established customs, attitudes, and opinions. Where segregation had been abolished in fact as well as in law, as in the Armed Forces, blacks would now question the intent and will of whites to eliminate covert discrimination. The Marine Corps in the decade of the 60s and the Vietnam War years was to be troubled deeply by racial incidents, some of them violent clashes, while it sought ways to promote better understanding between white and black Marines.

CHAPTER 7

THE VIETNAM ERA

An introduction to a changing philosophy among a vocal segment of blacks in America was furnished by Elijah Muhammed in a speech to an estimated 4,000 Black Muslims in New York on 31 July 1960. He called for the creation of an exclusively American black state either in the United States or in Africa and urged his followers to tell whites, "If we are going to live together, there must be a state for you, a state for us."[1] His separatist sentiments were by no means confined to his own religious sect; they found support among other charismatic black leaders pursuing their own courses of action. The cry for black separation, however, was but one small manifestation of an overall heightened black consciousness. This was everywhere apparent in demands for instruction in black history and culture in the public schools, in cultivation of certain aspects of African life in dress, music, and hair styling, and in a recognition of the values of a separate black life style best expressed in the phrase "black is beautiful." One must be careful, however, not "to equate the long overdue recognition by the Negro of his African beginnings with a repudiation of his American loyalties."[2]

The influence of this new awareness of individual and racial worth on the urban youth who furnished most black Marine Corps recruits was profound. If, as was frequently the case, their educational preparation for service life was deficient and their classification scores consequently low, their assignment to soft skill tasks was viewed as evidence of racial discrimination, not lack of qualification. The standards they were asked to meet were standards they saw as biased in favor of whites. Many of these young men, who in previous decades might have striven to change their life patterns, to emulate more successful whites and blacks, now felt no compulsion to meet such standards.

Integration, to the extent it meant equal opportunity and treatment was accepted, but integration in a social context was viewed in a different light by many young blacks. Their own life styles and values had more significance to them than those of others. These men were not ready to fit themselves into a behavior mold not of their own choosing. In a military environment, where there was a long-accepted pattern of what was correct conduct both on duty and off, a militant black would prove himself to be disruptive and highly visible. He could, and often did, obscure the fact that "the vast majority of black Marines that served in the Corps during the 60s and 70s were not militant and did not attack 'whitey'."[3]

The militants' attitude ran counter to that which had governed the service life of many of the veteran black Marine NCOs, men who had earned a respected place in the Corps based on individual achievement and performance. These men had experienced segregation at its demeaning worst, they had seen integration implemented as official policy, and they could see progress against discrimination. Imperfect though their situation might still be, these veteran black Marines had become a part of the Marine Corps "family." The outbreaks of racial tension and violence which were to mar the 60s decade in the Marine Corps would find these men ranged on the side of authority. In this respect, the veteran black Marines were in the mainstream of Marine Corps life, the militant younger blacks at times appeared to stand apart from it; neither group fully appreciated the others' background and attitudes. And yet they had a common cause, a need for full equality. One of the most striking aspects of this need, as seen by a perceptive young black officer:

> . . . was the recognition among the Negro community that before equality could be achieved, the Negro would have to change his image; both in his mind and in the mind of the white community. This image changing process was manifested in many ways: in patient example, in significant achievement, and in angry demands and rebellion.[4]

If mutual understanding between black men

wearing the same uniform was a vital necessity to the success of the Marine Corps mission, there was even more of a need for white Marines wearing that uniform to understand and accept the changing social order.

Action Against Discrimination

In June 1962, President John F. Kennedy appointed a President's Committee on Equal Opportunity in the Armed Forces headed by Gerhard A. Gesell, a prominent Washington attorney active in civil rights cases, with Nathaniel S. Colley, Abe Fortas, Louis J. Hector, Benjamin Muse, John S. Sengstacke, and Whitney M. Young, Jr. as members. The Gesell Committee's purpose was to investigate the status of minority groups, especially blacks, in the services and to see what progress had been made in the 14 years since President Truman had decreed the end of segregation in the Armed Forces. At virtually the same time, the Civil Rights Commission, through the Assistant Secretary of Defense (Manpower), requested Armed Forces cooperation in a study examining the status of blacks in uniform with respect to racial discrimination.[5] The resultant self examination by the Marine Corps did not turn up a completely clean bill of health, but it did show that many things had changed and for the better for black Marines. There were, however, signs in the summer of 1962 of restrictions in assignment practices; for instance, there were no black recruiters, no black women Marines at Parris Island, and there were several posts where blacks were not assigned because of off-base housing difficulties, among them Bridgeport, California; Charleston, South Carolina; and Hawthorne, Nevada.[6] The Gesell Committee found that: "Many of the Negroes in the Navy and Marine Corps are still grouped in assignments which perpetuate the image of the Negro as a menial or servant in respect to the total activities of these Services. . . ."[7]

In general, however, the initial report of the committee was complimentary of the efforts of the Armed Forces toward integration and equality. President Kennedy sent the report of Secretary of Defense Robert S. MacNamara on 21 June 1963 enjoining him to give it his "personal attention and action." The committee suggested measures to improve the effectiveness of current policies in the Armed Forces regarding equality of treatment and opportu-

Major Hurdle L. Maxwell, later the first black officer to command a Marine infantry battalion, visits a Vietnamese village in 1966. (USMC photo A419047).

nity. The Armed Forces were called upon to review their standards periodically "for promotion, selection, and assignment to make certain that latent ability is always properly measured and utilized."[8] Specific suggestions for better communication between commanding officers and their black personnel were made as well as suggestions for improving race relations on military bases.

Most strongly, the committee called for "a vigorous new program of action" to eliminate the "humiliation and degradation" suffered by black servicemen and their dependents in communities near the bases where they were required to serve. In regard to off-base housing, the report noted that: "Bad as the situation is for all personnel, it is much worse for Negroes who face discrimination in housing throughout the United States."[9] The formation of bi-racial community committees was encouraged to direct attention and offer solutions to problems of housing, transportation, education, recreational facilities, and community events, programs, and activities.

As an example, in Jacksonville, North Carolina, even before the Gesell Committee reported, Major General James P. Berkeley, commanding Camp Lejeune, and Colonel

Ernest C. Fuson, commanding the air facility at New River, had visited the mayor to inform him of the desire of the Secretary of the Navy that the city authorities "proceed in an orderly manner toward obtaining integration of all public and private facilities within the City of Jacksonville." [10] A mayor's bi-racial committee was formed and the help of influential businessmen and clergymen was solicited. By July 1963, Major General Alpha L. Bowser, the new Camp Lejeune commander, could report to General Berkeley that all the city's movie theaters were integrated as were restaurants and taverns. [11]

The power of commanding officers to restrict the offbase activities of military personnel undoubtedly accelerated the progress of integration in Jacksonville and in other similar cities and towns adjacent to military posts. Secretary MacNamara reinforced that power on 26 July 1963 with a directive which authorized the establishment of the Office of the Deputy Assistant Secretary of Defense (Civil Rights) and ordered the Services to use their authority to designate places "off limits" in combating discrimination. [12] The progressive enforcement of this policy was eventually to lead Secretary MacNamara to announce, on 7 September 1967, that the Department of Defense would declare "off limits" all segregated housing located near military installations throughout the United States. [13]

In another area of discrimination, public events, the Marine Corps took steps to curtail military participation and support of segregated activities. In a bulletin issued on 12 November 1963, commanding officers were directed to permit participation "only if the event was available to all persons without regard to race, creed, color or national origin." [14] In July 1964, the Secretary of the Navy issued a directive which further elaborated on military participation in public meetings which practised segregation or exclusion. The general policy stated was that: "The Department of Defense will not sponsor, support, or financially assist, directly or indirectly, any conference or meeting held under circumstances where participants are segregated or treated unequally because of race." [15]

Despite the various orders and directives enjoining discrimination both on and off base, there was a strong feeling among younger black Marines in the 60s that they were being discriminated against, particularly in the areas

Second Lieutenant Gloria Smith at her first duty station, Camp Pendleton in 1968. A captain in 1973, she was the senior black woman officer on active duty. (USMC Photo A557862).

of promotion, job assignment, and military justice. With only a handful of black officers and these mainly lieutenants and captains, there was almost a certainty that if a black got in trouble his judge would be white and if someone decided on his preference or performance of duty that person also would be white. If the decisions made were contrary to what the black Marine desired or thought he deserved, the accusation of racial prejudice came naturally to his mind. In this respect, he had the reinforcement of his own peer group of black Marines. It was quite easy to dismiss matters of comparative qualifications, needs of the service, and even responsibility for misdeeds in this atmosphere. More and more, some young black Marines tended to draw in upon themselves, to develop a brotherhood of racial pride, and to consider white Marines as inherently prejudiced against them. While white Marines for the most part, influenced by official directives and the outward evidences of desegregation and action against discrimination, considered that there was no racial inequality in the Marine Corps, many black Marines were not convinced.

Racial Turmoil

The 1960s was a period of increasing racial tension in the United States marked by a series of sit-ins, demonstrations, protest marches, and even riots as blacks strove to achieve the civil rights that long overdue laws and court decisions had given them. In many instances, the riotous confrontations were "generated," as the National Advisory Committee on Civil Disorders found, "out of an increasingly disturbed social atmosphere, in which typically a series of tension-heightening incidents over a period of weeks or months became linked in the minds of many in the Negro community with a reservior of underlying grievances." [16] The typical rioter was identified as a teenager or young adult, "proud of his race, extremely hostile to both whites and middle-class Negroes, and although informed about politics, highly distrustful of the political system." [17] Consider then that many men with this orientation were enlisted or drafted into the Marine Corps in the 1960s.

The stress and strains of American civilian society showed in the Birmingham, Alabama bus boycotts (1955–56) and in the confrontations over the educational rights of blacks at Little Rock, Arkansas (1957–58) and Oxford, Mississippi (1962–63). More serious incidents than these confrontations were riots in Philadelphia (1964). Watts (Los Angeles) (1965), and Detroit (1967). The year 1968 was a particularly bad year for violence with antiestablishment attitudes playing a significant part. A major incident was the assassination on 4 April in Memphis, Tennessee of Dr. Martin Luther King, the head of the Southern Christian Leadership Conference. The resulting tumultuous riots in Washington, Chicago, Los Angeles, and many other cities were marked by arson, looting, and loss of life.

This series of disturbances had its effect upon the Marine Corps also, which had a parallel rash of racially inspired confrontations of varying seriousness. In August 1968, Headquarters Marine Corps began compiling briefs on incidents within the Corps which might be considered as being basically racial. [18]

As one reviews these incidents, certain characteristics or patterns are observed. The locations were widespread—Vietnam, Okinawa, Japan, Hawaii, and various bases in the United States. Racial epithets were frequently "trigger words" for assaults. Many of the confrontations were between groups or gangs of 25–50 each. Sides were chosen on the basis of race with little apparent regard for the actual triggering incident itself. Many incidents were the result of gangs picking on individuals. Clubs and places of recreation were frequently the scenes of inciting episodes and drinking by one or more of the participants increased their belligerency accordingly.

Camp Lejeune became a focal point of concern about racial incidents in 1969, although it was by no means the only base where such incidents occurred. In the first eight months of the year, there were 160 reports of assaults, muggings, and robbery with racial overtones. [19] Major General Michael P. Ryan, commanding the 2d Marine Division stationed at the base, addressed himself to the problem on 9 April 1969 by forming a committee of seven officers to develop a paper on "the division's basic philosophy in addressing any minority group or discrimination problem . . . within the division." After an informal and limited exploration, a report was submitted on 23 April which made certain fairly specific criticisms:

> 1. That bigotry and prejudice were practised in the Corps and by white businessmen in the adjacent community.
> 2. That seniors placed obstructions in the way of young Marines seeking to grapple with the race problem.
> 3. That there was a failure to comply with the spirit and letter of the law.
> 4. That effective leadership was lacking. [20]

Acting with the report as a basis, General Ryan issued a division order on 27 June 1969 on the subject, "Fostering Unit Pride and Esprit Within the 2d Marine Division, FMF." [21] The order was accompanied by a Platoon Commander's Pamphlet dealing with the racial situation and equality of treatment and opportunity. It was a calm, reasoned approach to the racial situation, which discussed the contributory causes of friction, and outlined procedures by which complaints of discrimination could be handled.

In spite of this constructive attempt to create an atmosphere in which racial conflicts could be resolved, a serious incident occurred on the base less than a month after the order was issued. On 20 July, the night before the 1st Battalion, 6th Marines was to mount out to join the Sixth Fleet at Rota, Spain, a party was held at a service club adjacent to the battalion's barracks area. A mixed group of about 100 black and 75 white Marines were gathered to listen to the band hired for the occasion. During the course of the evening there were a number of minor flare ups that heightened tension. Then, at about 2240, shortly after most men had left the club to return to quarters, an "extremely bloody" white Marine burst into the club to say that he had been attacked by a group of black Marines. During the next half hour, 15 more white Marines were assaulted at six different locations by groups of black Marines. "The blacks were obviously in a high state of excitement, yelling, white beasts, call us niggers now, I'm the beast, look what I caught, we are going to mess up some beasts tonight, etc.' and were armed with broken broom handles and tree branches." [22] Many white Marines were unaware of trouble in the area and were taken by surprise. One white corporal later died of massive head injuries received as a result of a beating. At least two white Marines were stabbed and another hospitalized in a serious condition as a result of head injuries. [23]

Arrests were made and 44 men were charged; of this number, 24 had the charges dismissed, 5 were acquitted, and 13 were convicted of riot, disobedience, or assault. One man went absent without leave before the trial and the remaining black Marine was convicted of involuntary manslaughter and sentenced to nine years at hard labor. [24]

Following this incident, a House of Representatives sub-committee of the Armed Services Committee held hearings at Camp Lejeune and in Washington. From the 1,250 pages of testimony and supporting documents that it amassed, the subcommittee felt that it could enumerate the following as its findings:

1. The racial problem existing at Camp Lejeune is a reflection of the Nation's racial problem.

2. The average young black Marine has racial pride, drive for identity, and sensitivity to discrimination that is characteristic of the young black in the United States.

3. The Marine Corps and the other services have led the way and made substantial progress in integration of the races since 1948.

4. Racial differences and misunderstandings at Camp Lejeune can be attributed in large measure to lack of effective communication at the junior levels of command as well as vertically between the young Marine and his commander.

5. A shortage of mature leadership attributed in large measure to rapid buildup and turnover at the NCO and junior officer levels at Camp Lejeune has aggravated the racial problem.

6. There was a deterioration in discipline at Camp Lejeune.

7. The instances of permissiveness appearing at the junior levels of command are damaging to discipline but unfortunately mirror the society in which the young men live.

8. The security procedures at Camp Lejeune on the evening of July 20 were insufficient despite some warning of impending trouble.

9. Improved security measures are necessary at the ammunition storage areas and armories, as well as improved lighting in populated areas throughout the Camp Lejeune complex.

10. The fatality which occurred did not result from any misconduct on the part of the victim. [25]

The sub-committee reached a general conclusion that the disturbance "did not result from any specific provocation, but was generated by a few militant blacks who fanned the flames of racism, misconceptions, suspicions, and frustrations." The members felt that in identifying the root causes of race problems at Camp Lejeune they had also identified the root causes of similar problems that were typical of those at any military base. [26]

A short time prior to the release of the sub-committee's report in mid-December 1969, the Commandant, General Leonard F. Chapman, Jr., discussed the racial problems as he saw them following a two-week tour of commands in the Pacific and Southeast Asia. Highly significant were his remarks: "There is no question about it though, we've got a problem. We thought we had eliminated discrimination in the Marine Corps and we are still determined to do so. It is apparent from the last two weeks that we've not been as successful as we thought." [27] A riotous flareup at Kaneohe Bay between black and white Marines in August 1969 and instances of "fragging," tossing grenades into the tents and huts of white officers and NCOs, which occurred principally in rear areas in Vietnam, and repeated clashes between the races in the Koza City area on Okinawa all served to highlight the explosive situation.

The Commandant had taken steps to clarify the racial problems in the Marine Corps and to alleviate some of the causes of black dissatisfaction earlier in the year with the publication on 2 September 1969 of a directive dealing with "Racial Relations and Instances of Racial Violence within the Marine Corps." The following day he discussed his message with representatives of the press. In the directive, General Chapman commented that the recent instances of racial violence had almost been unheard of among Marines in combat but appeared to have taken place as they moved to other areas or returned to the United States. He emphatically stated that acts of violence between Marines "can not be tolerated, and must stop."

He then proceeded to lay down a series of guiding steps in handling racial difficulties in the Corps, stressing that "the causes of friction, rather than the symptoms, must be identified by all commanders, frankly and openly discussed, and eliminated where possible." He affirmed his support of traditional high standards of military appearance, military courtesy, and proficiency in the Marine Corps.[28]

In specific reference to the Afro/natural haircut long desired by many black Marines, he stated simply that commanders would permit it "providing it conforms with current Marine Corps regulations." In his press conference, the Commandant quoted the regulations: "Hair shall always be worn neatly and closely trimmed. It shall be clipped at the sides and back so as to present an evenly graduated appearance. The hair on top must not be over three inches in length. Long and conspicuous sideburns are prohibited."

General Chapman also dealt with what has been called the black power salute (the raising of a clenched fist). He reminded Marines that "no actions, signs, symbols, gestures, and words which are contrary to tradition will be permitted during formations or when rendering military courtesies to colors, the national anthem, or individuals." He noted however, that "individual signs between groups of individuals will be accepted for what they are—gestures of recognition and unity. . . ."[30]

The Commandant gave as one of the purposes of his directive his desire "to impress on all my commanders the absolute necessity of total impartiality for any consideration whatever based on race or creed or religion." He stressed that the Marine Corps had not and would not tolerate discrimination nor would it relax the firm, impartial discipline that had always been its standard.[31]

Black Officer Procurement and Human Relations [32]

There were many steps that the Marine Corps took in the late 60s to alleviate the tense racial situation in its ranks, but central to all the proposed and enacted programs was an intensive effort to increase the number of black officers. In May 1967 when the Assistant Secretary of Defense (Manpower) recommended to the Commandant that the Corps double the number of its black officers, there were 155 serving on active duty out of total officer strength of approximately 23,000.[33] Major Kenneth H. Berthoud, Jr. (an officer selected for lieutenant colonel) was ordered to Headquarters Marine Corps following a tour in Vietnam to become the Special Advisor to the Deputy Chief of Staff (Manpower) for Minority Officer Procurement. He was charged with the coordination of procurement activities within the Marine Corps and with interested outside agencies.

A series of steps to energize the program was proposed by a study group at Headquarters and approved by the Commandant in October. The thrust of these proposals was to increase the visibility of black Marines, particularly black officers, to the black community by exposure in all kinds of media, to assign black officers as officer selection officers to make contact with black college men and women, and to make an extensive effort to find black enlisted men who had the qualifications to become officers. The first six black officers assigned to officer selection duties were: Captains Delmas A. Costin (1st Marine Corps District); George H. Walls, Jr. (4th); Tommy D. Gregory (6th); Merlon Hughes (8th); Ramon A. Johnson (9th); and Solomon P. Hill (12th).[34]

One of the first outside agencies that Lieutenant Colonel Berthoud contacted in his efforts to find suitable officer candidates was the Montford Point Marine Association (MPMA). This organization, primarily of black Marines and former Marines but with a membership open to all, had been formed in 1965 when a group of approximately 300 men who had served at Montford Point gathered at Philadelphia's Adelphi Hotel in August to hold a reunion and relive their experiences. It was a happy and memorable occasion and as one participant recalled:

> . . . every time the elevator doors would open on the ballroom floor, the enthusiastic greeting "Baby" could be heard, even on the street, three floors down; and men who hadn't seen each other for 20 or 22 years would warmly embrace. This scene was repeated many times for two full days.[35]

Now a thriving nationally chartered veterans' organization with chapters in many cities, the Montford Point Marine Association consistently supported the black officer procurement effort. Intensely proud of those black Marines who had become officers, the association's members were enthusiastic about the effort to increase the number of officers and were well aware through contact with young black veterans of how vital the need was for a stronger representation of blacks among the Marine Corps leaders. It was "of paramount importance," as Major Edward L. Green, the first black Marine instructor to be assigned to the faculty of the Naval Academy (1968), observed, "to correct the under-

Lieutenant Colonel Kenneth H. Berthoud, Special Advisor for Minority Officer Procurement, is awarded the Navy Commendation Medal with combat "V" for his service in Vietnam in 1966–67 by Major General Raymond G. Davis, Assistant Chief of Staff (G–1) at Headquarters Marine Corps. (USMC Photo A415451)

representation of blacks in the officer structure of the services. Until we achieve an adequate black officer distribution throughout the command and policy-making levels, the basic fairness of the entire institution will remain in doubt." [36]

Major Green, who taught military law and leadership, introduced the first formal instruction in race relations at the academy, served as co-chairman of its Human Relations Advisory Council, and was instrumental in recruiting a number of black officers during his three-year tour of duty. Eight of the 12 black midshipmen in the class of 1972 joined the Marine Corps.[37] Similar dedicated efforts by Lieutenant Colonel Berthoud and his successors, Lieutenant Colonel Frank E. Petersen, Jr. and Major Solomon P. Hill, and the young black captains assigned to officer procurement duties helped the number of black officers on active duty to grow appreciably. On 30 September 1973, there were 378 black officers, 367 men and 11 women, 2.03 percent of the total number of Marine officers on active duty.[38] Since the primary target of officer procurement is the college graduate, competition from business, industry, and the other Services was tough. Although the number has increased slowly, less than five percent of the black male population is college educated. It is not likely, therefore, that the percentage of black Marine officers will soon approximate that of black

people in the United States, about 12 percent, or blacks enlisted in the Marine Corps, 17.41 percent on 30 September 1973 (29,839 men and 341 women.) [39]

What has happened, however, to balance this lack of numbers is a far greater awareness within the Marine Corps among the white majority and the various minority racial groups of each others' backgrounds, aspirations, and life styles. This has come about as the result of a formally structured program of human relations training that affects all Marines from generals to privates.

The program had its origin in the recommendations of a 17-month study done by the American Institutes of Research of Washington of the inter-racial situation in the Marine Corps. The research teams visited six major bases in the United States and conducted extensive interviews with Marines of every race and rank. They found that most Marines believed that inter-racial hostilities within the Corps were a reflection of similar feelings in American society and that these attitudes came into the Marine Corps with the individual Marine. They also found that the use of racial and ethnic epithets and the lack of understanding that their use indicated was a pervading problem. One investigator noted: "Marines, both black and white, told us they were most bothered by being called nigger, kike, wop, honkie, and other names by Marines they lived and worked with." [40] In its report of 10 November 1971, the research institution recommended the establishment of a formal human relations course to be given to all Marines presented through a live discussion method guided by extensively trained instructors. The objective of the recommended program was to ensure through education more constructive relationships between Marines and between Marines and people outside the Marine Corps.

As a result of the findings of the study as it progressed and decisions at the Department of Defense level that all Services should initiate some form of schooling to improve racial relations, the Marine Corps took a number of steps to improve its grasp of the situation, including the organization in 1969 of an Equal Opportunity Branch at Headquarters to assist in the formulation of plans, policies, and programs "that would ensure that all Marines regardless of race, color, creed, or national origin are treated equally." [41] The post of Special Assist-

Sergeant Brenda Good, a human relations instructor, guides a discussion group of Marines from Headquarters Battalion, FMFPac. (Photo from Human Affairs Division, HQ, FMFPac).

ant to the Commandant for Minority Affairs was created and initially filled by Lieutenant Colonel Frank E. Petersen, Jr., then the Corps' senior black regular officer, who was later succeeded in 1972 by Major Edward L. Green, following his tour at the Naval Academy. The job, as it evolved, was that of trouble shooter, liaison officer, presentor, and, basically, advisor to the Commandant on the fundamentals of minority problems and how their solutions were working.

A Marine Corps Human Relations Institute was formally established at the Marine Corps Recruit Depot, San Diego on 1 July 1972 to train instructors for the human relations program and to evaluate the effectiveness of the program at all organizational levels. Even before the first official class of officers and enlisted men was graduated, however, 47 instruc-

tors had been trained who were out in the field training others in the techniques of managing human relations seminars which were to be required of all Marines. The initial goal was that every Marine, regardless of his rank, was to have 20 hours of instruction and participation in these sessions and that such involvement was to be an annual affair. The new Commandant, General Robert E. Cushman, Jr., expressed the intent of the program in a letter to all general officers and commanding officers on 6 June 1972:

Our Corps is in the front line of the Nation's effort to improve the areas of understanding and cooperation among all Americans. I view our human relations efforts as major steps in helping the Corps to attain that environment of equal opportunity, understanding, brotherhood, and professionalism so vital to our future effectiveness. That environment, when combined with an open, two-way channel of communication among all Marines, will permit us to devote our total energies toward maintaining what our Nation needs and expects from us, a combat-ready Corps of Marines.[42]

In no sense were the human relation seminars intended to be "rap sessions" or undisciplined occasions for the airing of personal grievances. They were and are structured learning sessions with a purposeful cross-section of all ranks and races brought together in small groups to develop understanding and tolerance of each others' background and point of view. General Cushman assessed the purpose of the program after a little over a year of its operation in an address to the members of the National Newspaper Publishers Association in Houston, Texas on 21 June 1973. He observed:

> Each new Marine we get—whether officer or enlisted—brings along, figuratively speaking, his own personal seabag filled with the prejudices he has been collecting for eighteen years or more. The simple act of putting on a green uniform does not cause him to empty that seabag. But through training we try to instill the desire in him to *repack* that seabag—discarding the harmful preferences and prejudices—so it does both him and fellow Marines the most good.[43]

In their attempts to solve the racial problems of the Marine Corps, Generals Chapman and Cushman called upon the advice of a Commandant's Advisory Committee for Minority Affairs. Originally, General Chapman asked Mr. Hobart Taylor, Jr., a prominent black attorney in Washington, to investigate the racial situation in the Marine Corps. After two fact-finding trips as the Commandant's representative, one to Camp Lejeune on 22–23 June 1970 and another to Okinawa from 15–22 November, Mr. Taylor recommended that an advisory committee of interested and concerned civilians be formed.[44] His suggestion was approved by the Commandant on 6 January 1971. A list of potential members was submitted for consideration on 12 April by the Equal Opportunity Branch and the final list of original members was approved in June. The first meeting of the committee was held on 6 August 1971.

Mr. Taylor served as committee chairman and the initial members included Richard A. Beaumont, W. Leonard Evans, Jr., Jose C. Gomez, Robert R. Gros, E. T. Guerrero, E. Frederick Marrow, A. B. Trowbridge, and

The Honorable Hobart Taylor, Jr. signs the guest book at Marine Barracks, Washington, after being presented the Navy Distinguished Public Service Award for his service as Chairman, Commandant's Committee on Minority Affairs. Looking on is First Sergeant Lee M. Bradley. (USMC Photo 4705912).

Richard L. Vaughn. The committee was later enlarged by the addition of Dr. Lewis C. Dowdy. The members included lawyers, bankers, educators, blacks and whites, many of whom had held responsible positions in government. The committee's basic charter was "to advise on ways to bring effectively the true policy of the Marine Corps for equal opportunity to minority groups, ease racial tensions, and improve minority relations."[45]

The members, individually and collectively, made a number of trips to various Marine bases in early 1972, speaking to all manner of Marines and setting a pattern for later similar inspection trips. They found, among other things, that many black Marines doubted the sincerity of the budding human relations program and that they felt that the military justice system was harsher on blacks than others. But as one member noted the Marine Corps was far ahead of private industry in its openness, willingness to be examined, and in its actions in regard to improving race relations.[46]

Perhaps the crux of the race relations issue in the Marine Corps had been expressed earlier by Lieutenant General Keith B. McCutcheon, while he was commanding the III Marine Amphibious Force in Vietnam. In a 16 October 1970 article in *Sea Tiger*, the force's weekly newspaper, he had, drawing on his own experience in fighting a personal bout with cancer, pointed out:

> Like human cancer this problem of racial minorities can have two outcomes. It can kill us if we don't operate soon enough. It can make us even stronger as a Corps and a nation if we face facts now and solve it. Let's continue to move out toward that end, but do so as mature, reasonable men in a sane, peaceful, nonviolent manner.[47]

Vietnam

While United States military assistance to South Vietnam dates back to 1954, it was not until the spring of 1962 that Marine Corps helicopters were deployed to that country to support the South Vietnamese in their battles with the Viet Cong. It was March 1965 before Marine ground forces, the infantry battalions, artillery batteries, and tank platoons of the 9th Marine Expeditionary Brigade, were committed to defend the air base at Da Nang. Further ground troops and aircraft squadrons followed as the tempo of the fighting and the extent of American involvement increased. The III Marine Amphibious Force (III MAF), which controlled all American forces in the northern five provinces of South Vietnam, grew in strength until it included over 85,000 Marines in 1968, at the height the American commitment.

After major troop withdrawals began in September 1969, the South Vietnamese armed forces assumed an increasingly greater share of the fighting. In June 1971, the last Marine combat troops, the 3d Marine Amphibious Brigade, departed Da Nang. Marine aircraft groups returned to Vietnam temporarily in 1972 to support the South Vietnamese against resurgent North Vietnamese invaders, but these units were out of the country by the end of the year.[48] Over 448,000 Marines served in Vietnam between 1965 and 1973; of this number approximately 41,000 were black Marines.[49]

From the first commitment of troops until the last, black Marines were always present in Vietnam. To an even greater extent than in the Korean War, the identity of black effort as something apart from the total combat and combat support effort of all Marines is virtually impossible. Certainly there were individual heroics and accomplishments which can be cited, but in essence the Marine Corps' contribution to the fighting was a team contribution and black Marines were an integral part of the team. There were racial incidents and confrontations in rear areas in Vietnam, but these disruptions did not extend to the sectors of fighting, where the color of a man's skin was of no import to his role as a combat Marine.

Squads, platoons, and companies were led in battle by black officers and NCOs. Responsible staff and support positions were held by blacks throughout III MAF. Black pilots flew close air support for the Marines and South Vietnamese on the ground and ranged north over the demilitarized zone in attacks on North Vietnamese military targets. Symbolic of the positions of trust given to black Marines were the Vietnam roles of the Corps' then senior regular black officer and NCO, Lieutenant Colonel Frank E. Petersen, Jr. and Sergeant Major Edgar R. Huff.

Lieutenant Colonel Petersen reached Vietnam in May 1968 after having served as the operations officer of the Marine Reserve Training Detachment at Willow Grove, Pennsylvania. He became the commanding officer of Marine Fighter Attack Squadron (VMFA) 314, a Phantom jet unit operating out of Chu Lai air base. Petersen was the first black to command a tactical air squadron in the Navy or the Marine Corps. While he had the squadron (May 1968-February 1969), VMFA-314 received the 1968 Hanson Award as the best fighter squadron in the Marine Corps. During his service as commanding officer and squadron pilot, Lieutenant Colonel Petersen was shot down and rescued and added over 280 combat missions to his total from Korea. He also added a Legion of Merit, a Purple Heart, and the Combat Action Ribbon to his personal decorations for this Vietnam service.[50]

Sergeant Major Huff, like many black regulars, served two tours of duty in Vietnam. Originally arriving at Da Nang in May 1967 after serving as base sergeant major at Camp Pendleton, he was assigned duties as sergeant major of the 1st Military Police Battalion of the Force Logistic Command. In January 1968, during a fire fight with an enemy infiltrating force, he was severely wounded while rescuing a radioman trapped in an open field by enemy fire. Recommended for the Silver Star for his heroic actions, he eventually received the Bronze Star and two Purple Hearts for his wounds. In May 1968, when the sergeant major of III MAF was wounded during an

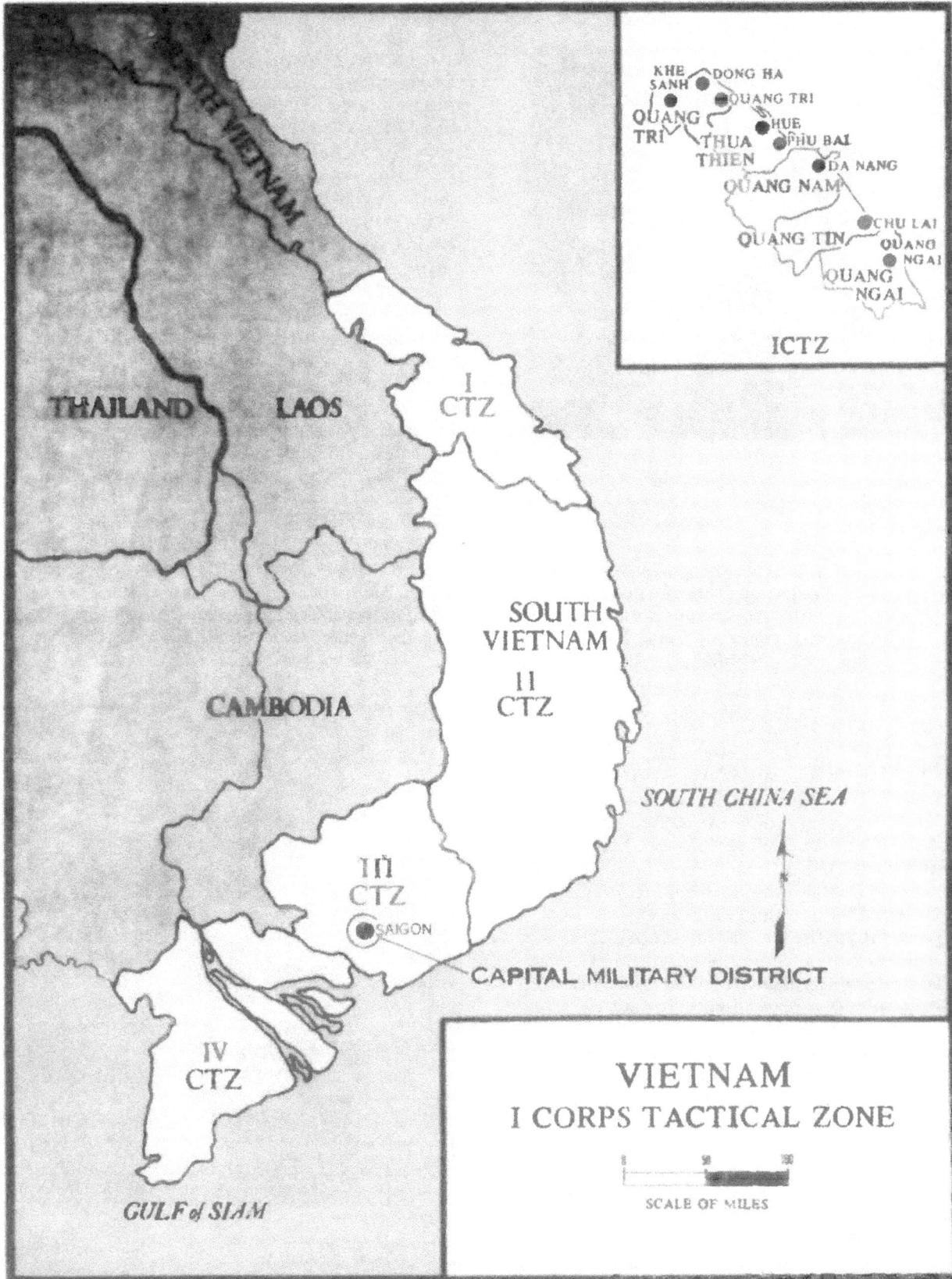

KHE SANH
DONG HA
QUANG TRI
QUANG TRI
HUE
THUA THIEN
PHU BAI
DA NANG
QUANG NAM
CHU LAI
QUANG TIN
QUANG NGAI
QUANG NGAI

ICTZ

SOUTH VIETNAM

THAILAND

LAOS

I CTZ

SOUTH VIETNAM

II CTZ

CAMBODIA

SOUTH CHINA SEA

III CTZ

SAIGON

CAPITAL MILITARY DISTRICT

IV CTZ

GULF of SIAM

VIETNAM
I CORPS TACTICAL ZONE

SCALE OF MILES

Leading his platoon in an operation south of Da Nang in March 1967 is Staff Sergeant Percy J. Price, former military heavyweight boxing champion. (USMC Photo A370016).

enemy rocket attack on force headquarters, Huff as the next senior sergeant major in III MAF was appointed force sergeant major by the commanding general, then Lieutenant General Robert E. Cushman, Jr. Although he only held the position for a month while he finished his Vietnam tour, Huff was back again in October 1970 to serve as III MAF sergeant major after two years as the sergeant major of the 2d Marine Aircraft Wing at Cherry Point. By now the senior sergeant major in the Marine Corps in point of service in grade, Huff served successively under Lieutenant Generals Keith B. McCutcheon and Donn J. Robertson and witnessed the withdrawal of III MAF from Vietnam to Okinawa.[51]

Symbolic of the pervasive combat presence of black Marines in Vietnam was the fact that the senior enlisted Marine in the epic battle for Khe Sanh was a black man who had first reported as a recruit to Montford Point on 8 April 1943. During the North Vietnamese Tet offensive in the early months of 1968, Sergeant Major Agrippa W. Smith of the 1st Battalion, 9th Marines was omnipresent in his unit's positions at the embattled combat base. "Gripper" Smith's battalion was attached to the 26th Marines, the regiment charged with defending the strategic northern outpost.

When the decision was made to award the regiment and its reinforcing units the Presidential Unit Citation for their outstanding

combat performance, Sergeant Major Smith was choosen to accompany the regimental commander, Colonel David E. Lownds, and the regimental colors back to Washington. In a much-publicized ceremony at the White House on 23 May 1968, President Lyndon B. Johnson placed the citation streamer on the colors of the 26th, proudly borne by Sergeant Major Smith.[52] On his return to Vietnam in June 1968, Smith, who was awarded the Bronze Star for his part in the Khe Sanh battle, fittingly became the sergeant major of the 26th Marines.[53]

There is no way of calculating the number of decorations earned by black Marines in the Vietnam War: Navy Crosses, Silver Stars, Distinguished Flying Crosses, Bronze Stars, and a host of other medals were won by these men for heroic action and meritorious service. In one category of awards, however, there is no doubt about who and how many were the recipients.

Five black Marines were awarded the Medal of Honor during the Vietnam fighting, each man for "conspicuous gallantry and intrepidity at the risk of his life above and beyond the call of duty." All used their own bodies in the thick of a fire fight to shield the blast and fragments

Lieutenant Colonel Frank E. Petersen, Jr., Commanding Officer, Marine Fighter Attack Squadron 314, climbs into his Phantom jet for a combat mission in 1968. (USMC Photo A422355).

His platoon leader rushes to the assistance of Corporal Mitchell Smith, machine gunner with Company M, 3d Battalion, 7th Marines, during a fire fight with Viet Cong in 1966. (USMC photo A369436).

of enemy grenades from their comrades; all perished in the selfless attempts. On 28 February 1967, during operations in the jungle northwest of Cam Lo, the first black Marine earned his country's highest decoration. He was PFC James Anderson, Jr. of Compton, California, a rifleman with Company F, 2d Battalion, 3d Marines. Later that year, on 6 September, Sergeant Rodney M. Davis of Macon, Georgia, a platoon guide in Company B, 1st Battalion, 5th Marines sacrificed his life for his men during heavy fighting in Quang Nam Province. PFC Ralph H. Johnson of Charleston, South Carolina, on 5 March 1968, while serving as a scout with Company A, 1st Reconnaissance Battalion deep in enemy territory, saved the life of one of his comrades at the cost of his own. On 23 February 1969, PFC Oscar P. Austin of Phoenix, Arizona, an assistant machine gunner with Company E, 2d Battalion, 7th Marines was killed while protecting a wounded man from enemy grenades and rifle fire. The fifth black Marine to be awarded the Medal of Honor was PFC Robert H. Jenkins, Jr. of Interlachen, Florida for actions while serving as a machine gunner with Company C, 3d Reconnaissance Battalion on 5 March 1969 in the defense of Fire Support Base Argonne south of the demilitarized zone.[54]

Conclusion

Throughout the troubled years of the Vietnam War, new black Marines did their duty in combat, but a significant minority could not reconcile themselves to the Corps as they found it outside of battle. Since they were part of American society, they carried into the

President Lyndon B. Johnson shakes hand with Sergeant Major Agrippa W. Smith after a ceremony awarding the Presidential Unit Citation to the 26th Marines for heroic action at Khe Sanh in 1968. Looking on is Colonel David E. Lownds, who commanded the regiment. (USMC Photo A416505).

Marine Corps "prejudices felt by all Americans;"[55] in this respect they were no different than their white comrades in arms. Victims of discrimination in civilian life, the young blacks were suspicious of the military system in which they found themselves and quick to find or infer discriminatory practices. Their militancy in advocating what they considered their just rights and their sometimes abrasive projection of black solidarity introduced a new element of concern to leaders of the Marine Corps. It was realized early in the 1960s that the *status quo* of life in the Corps was unalterably shaken by events taking place outside its confines. It was quite evident that there was no room for complacency about the racial situation and that strong and effective measures to alleviate a challenging problem would have to be taken. And they were. The thrust of this effort was toward the complete elimination of discrimination, even "the appearance, however unintentional, of discrimination."[56] Coupled with this insistence on equality of opportunity was an ongoing Corps-wide program to promote mutual understanding of the other man's point of view.

All this was a far cry from the situation that faced the first black Marines who reported to Montford Point Camp in August 1942. Joining a segregated Marine Corps that did not want them, these men won themselves a proud niche in Marine Corps history. They proved they could wear the Marine uniform with honor, that they could persevere in the face of adversity, and that they could hold up their heads to their family and friends and say, "I am somebody and I have done something."[57] These pioneer black Marines won the way for others that followed; what they did proved there was a place, an important place, for blacks in the Marine Corps.

The first black Marine to complete 30 years of regular service retired on 28 September 1972. His military life spanned the dark years of segregation and the gradual advance toward integration to the present climate of human awareness. When Sergeant Major Huff ended his active duty years, he summed up a varied and honored career with a simple oft-repeated statement: "The Marine Corps has been good to me and I feel I have been good to the Marine Corps." [58] There can be no better yardstick by which to evaluate the worth of the Corps to black Marines and their worth in return than that philosophy, for good measure received, good measure given.

The grand old man in the history of black Marines would have to be Sergeant Major Gilbert H. "Hashmark" Johnson. Tough as nails when he presided over the recruit drill field at Montford Point and imbued throughout his career with a driving ambition for black Marines to succeed, to be somebody, he mellowed somewhat in later life to the status of elder statesman and spokesman for a generation of men who led the way toward desegregation and the end of discrimination in the Marine Corps. He died, stricken by a heart attack, while addressing a testimonial dinner of the Camp Lejeune Chapter of the Montford Point Marine Association on 5 August 1972. His topic, typically, was the history of the MPMA and blacks in the Marine Corps. [59] There could have been no man prouder of the accomplishments of black Marines, and perhaps no man who left such a personal mark on others through his insistence that the first of his race in the Corps would "measure up." It was altogether fitting, therefore, that his name was commemorated in the Marine Corps

Sergeant Major Edgar R. Huff, who retired in 1972 after 30 years service, having held the rank of sergeant major longer than any Marine on active duty. (USMC Photo A135412).

where it first began to be known. On the recommendation of the Executive Board of the MPMA, endorsed by Assistant Secretary of the Navy James E. Johnson, himself a Montford Pointer, the Commandant, General Cushman, approved the renaming of Montford Point Camp. [60] On 19 April 1974, in ceremonies at Camp Lejeune, Camp Gilbert H. Johnson was activated at Montford Point. [61] This well-deserved tribute to a distinguished human being honors every black man and woman who has worn the Marine uniform, as he did, with pride of self and Corps.

APPENDIX A

NOTES

Introduction

[1] Louis F. Middlebrook. *History of Maritime Connecticut during the American Revolution. 1775–1783*, 2 vols. (Salem, Mass.: Essex Institute. 1925). I, p. 26, 118–120; *Massachusetts Soldiers and Sailors of the Revolutionary War*, 17 vols. (Boston, 1896–1908), V, p. 879, XIV, p. 955; *Pennsylvania Archives*, 2d Series, Vol. I, pp. 296–97.

[2] John Elliot ltr to James Read. dtd 24 November 1778 (John Paul Jones Papers. Library of Congress).

[3] Facsimile copy in Reference Section, History and Museums Division, Headquarters Marine Corps of original held by Pennsylvania Historical Society (hereafter RefSec, Hist&Mus Div. HQMC).

[4] Office of Naval Records and Library, *Naval Documents Related to the Quasi-War between the United States and France: Naval Operations from February 1797 to October 1798*, 7 vols. (Washington, 1935–1938), I, p. 41.

[5] Maj William Ward Burrows ltr to Lt John Hall, dtd 8 September 1798 (Chronology File, 1798—RefSec, Hist&Mus Div, HQMC).

[6] Col Cyril Field, RMLI, *Britain's Sea Soldiers*, 2 vols. (Liverpool: The Lyceum Press. 1924) I, p. 26

[7] Navy Department, *Regulations, Circulars, Orders & Decisions, for the Guide of Officers of the Navy of the United States* (Washington: C. Alexander. 1851), p. 6.

[8] Dennis D. Nelson, *The Integration of the Negro into the U. S. Navy* (New York: Farrar, Straus and Young. 1951), p. 11.

Chapter 1—A Chosen Few

Unless otherwise noted, the material in this chapter is derived from: Muster rolls of the units stationed at Montford Point Camp, Aug42—Jul43 (RefSec, Hist&MusDiv, HQMC); SgtMaj Gilbert H. Johnson interview with Hist Div, dtd 27–28 Jun72 (Oral History Collection, Hist&Mus Div, HQMC), hereafter *G. H. Johnson interview*; Sgt Maj Edgar R. Huff interview with Hist Div, dtd 26–28 Jun72 (Oral History Collection, Hist&Mus Div, HQMC), hereafter *Huff interview*; *Montford Point, Camp Lejeune, New River, North Carolina* (Philadelphia: Campus Publishing Company, c. 1943), hereafter *Montford Point Pictorial*. The chapter title was decided upon before the authors were aware of the existence of a novel of black Marines' experience in the late 1940s, *A Chosen Few* by Hari Rhodes (Bantam Books, 1965). A copy of the book was donated to the History and Museums Division Library by Mr. Joseph Carpenter.

[1] From the original draft of Sgt Edward J. Evans "Men of Montford Point" (Negro Marines—Published Articles, Subject File, RefSec, Hist&Mus Div, HQMC).

[2] MajGen Thomas Holcomb testimony in Hearings of the General Board of the Navy, dtd 23Jan42, Subj: "Enlistment of Men of Colored Race (201)" (Operational Archives Branch, Naval Historical Center), p. 18.

[3] *Ibid.*, p. 15.

[4] *Ibid.*

[5] *Ibid.*, p. 18.

[6] R. L. Lapica, ed., *Facts on File Yearbook—1942* (New York: Persons Index on File, Inc., 1943), p. 91M, hereafter cited as *Facts on File*, preceded by the year and followed by page location.

[7] 1942 *Facts on File*, p. 109A.

[8] Navy Department Press and Radio Release, dtd 20May42 (Negro Marines Press Releases, Subject File, RefSec, His&MusDiv, HQMC).

[9] Gen Ray A. Robinson interview with HistDiv, dtd 18–19 Mar68 (Oral History Collection, Hist Div, HQMC).

[10] Excerpt from Evans, "Men of Montford Point," *op. cit.*

[11] LtCol Frank O. Hough, Maj Verle E. Ludwig, and Henry I. Shaw, Jr., *Pearl Harbor to Guadalcanal—History of U. S. Marine Corps Operations in World War II*, Vol. I (Washington: Historical Branch, G-3 Division, Headquarters U. S. Marine Corps, 1958), pp. 78–83, 223–224.

[12] "Col Cockrell Suceeds Col Woods as CO at MP," in *Camp Lejeune Globe*, dtd 6Sep44, p. 2.

[13] *G. H. Johnson interview.*

[14] Col Samuel A. Woods, Jr., memo to Director, Division of Plans and Policies, dtd 21Apr42 (File 2385/40–51, 51st Composite Defense Battalion, Central Files, HQMC).

[15] *Ibid.*

[16] CMC ltr to OIC, Eastern, Central, and Southern Recruiting Divisions, dtd 15May42 (File 2385/40–51, 51st Composite Defense Battalion, Central Files, HQMC).

[17] *Huff interview.*

[18] Mr. Obie Hall interview with HistDiv, dtd 16Aug72 (Oral History Collection, Hist&MusDiv, HQMC), hereafter *Hall interview*.

[19] CMC to Prospective CO, 51st, dtd 14Aug42 (File 2385/40–51, 51st Composite Defense Battalion, Central Files, HQMC).

[20] Col Theodore A. Holdahl Officer's Case File (Manpower Department, HQMC).

[21] *G. H. Johnson interview.*

[22] Battery A, 51st Composite Defense Battalion Muster Roll, Aug42.

[23] CMC ltr to CO, 51st Composite Defense Battalion, dtd 9Oct42 (File 2385/40–51, 51st Composite Defense Battalion, Central Files, HQMC).

[24] CMC memo to CO, 51st Composite Defense Battalion, dtd 19Dec42, Subj: "51st Composite Defense Battalion" (File 2385/40–51, 51st Composite Defense Battalion, Central Files, HQMC).

[25] *G. H. Johnson interview.*

[26] *Huff interview.*

[27] *G. H. Johnson interview.*

[28] Personal data sheets on SgtMaj Charles F. Anderson and 1stSgt Charles W. Simmons (Negro Marine Officers, Subject File, RefSec, Hist&MusDiv, HQMC).

[29] *Norfolk Journal and Guide*, dtd 9Mar46.

[30] Director, Division of Plans and Policies memo to CMC, dtd 29 Oct 42, subj: "Enlistment of Colored personnel in the Marine Corps Reserve" (File 2385/40–51, 51st Composite Defense Battalion, Central Files, HQMC).

[31] M–1 Section, Division of Plans and Policies memo to Chief of Naval Personnel, dtd 8Mar43, subj: "Procurement of colored personnel through Selective Service" (Negroes in the Armed Services File, Central Files, HQMC).

[32] Col Samuel A. Woods, Jr., memo to Director, Division of Plans and Policies, subj: "Colored Personnel" (File 2385/40–51, 51st Composite Defense Battalion, Central Files, HQMC).

[33] Mr. David C. Hendricks interview with HistDiv, dtd 7Jun72; Mr. Herman Darden, Jr., interview with HistDiv, dtd 15Aug72, hereafter *Darden interview* (Oral History Collection, HistDiv, HQMC).

[34] CO, Montford Point Camp ltr to CMC, dtd 19May43, Subj: "Colored Personnel, Weekly Report" (Copy in Negro Marines, Subject File, RefSec, Hist&MusDiv, HQMC).

[35] Col William B. Onley Officer's Case File (Manpower Department, HQMC).

[36] Maj Albert O. Madden Officer's Case File (Manpower Department, HQMC).

[37] MGySgt Frederic H. Clayton interview with HistDiv, ca. 15Sep72.

[38] *G. H. Johnson interview.*

[39] Hendricks interview, *op. cit.*

[40] *Huff interview.*

[41] SgtMaj Gilbert H. Johnson remarks at a meeting of the Camp Lejeune Chapter, Montford Point Marine Association, ca. 1967 (Negro Marines, Subject File, RefSec, Hist&MusDiv, HQMC).

[42] *G. H. Johnson interview; Hall interview.*

[43] CMC remarks at Montford Point Marine Association's 25th Anniversary Testimonial Dinner, Sheraton Park Hotel, Washington, D. C., dtd 20Apr68 (CMC Speech File, RefSec, Hist&MusDiv, HQMC).

[44] *Huff interview*, Clayton interview, *op. cit.*; Mr. Alex Johnson interview with HistDiv, dtd 16Aug72, hereafter *A. Johnson interview* (Oral History Collection, Hist&MusDiv, HQMC).

Chapter 2—The 51st Defense Battalion

Unless otherwise noted, the material in this chapter is derived from: Muster Rolls of the 51st Composite Defense Battalion, Aug42-Jun43 and the 51st Defense Battalion, Jun43-Jan46; 51st Defense Battalion War Diary, Apr 44-Aug45; Detachment A, 51st Defense Battalion War Diary, Mar-Jul44; *Darden interview; Hall interview*.

[1] LtCol Floyd A. Stephenson Officer's Case File (Manpower Department, HQMC).

[2] Commanding Officer, 51st Composite Battalion ltr to CMC, dtd 5 May 1943, Subj: Change of Organization, 51st Composite Defense Battalion (2385/40–51 File, 51st Composite Defense Battalion, Central Files, HQMC).

[3] *Ibid.*, 1st Endorsement by Col Samuel A. Woods, Jr., dtd 7 May 1943.

[4] CMC ltr to Commanding Officer, Montford Point Camp, dtd 28 May 1943, Subj: Change of Organization, 51st Composite Defense Battalion (2385/40–51 File, 51st Composite Defense Battalion, Central Files, HQMC).

[5] T/O E–410, Defense Battalion, approved 25 June 1943 (RefSec, Hist&MusDiv, HQMC).

[6] LtCol Floyd A. Stephenson ltr to CMC, dtd 30 May 1944, Subj: 51st Defense Battalion, Fleet Marine Force (Negroes in the Armed Forces File, Central Files, HQMC), hereafter *Stephenson letter*.

[7] News Release, Public Relations Office, Camp Lejeune, Sep43 (Negro Marines, Press Release File, RefSec, Hist&MusDiv, HQMC); Casualty Card of Cpl Gilbert Fraser, Jr. (RefSec, Hist&MusDiv, HQMC).

[8] *Stephenson letter.*

[9] *Darden interview.*

[10] "Flashes from 51st," *New River Poineer*, dtd 16Sep43, p. 8. (RefSec, Hist&MusDiv, HQMC).

[11] *Hall interview.*

[12] *Stephenson letter.*

[13] CO, 51st DefBn ltr to CMC, dtd 20Jul44, Subj: Combat Efficiency, 51st DefBn (Negroes in the Armed Forces File, Central Files, HQMC).

[14] LtCol Floyd A. Stephenson ltr to CMC, dtd 25Sep 44, Subj: 51st DefBn, circumstances attending its departure from Camp Lejeune, N. C., and combat efficency of (Negroes in the Armed Forces File, Central Files, HQMC), hereafter *Stephenson letter II*.

[15] *Hall interview.*

[16] *Stephenson letter.*

[17] Dr. Charles W. Simmons ltr to DirMCHist&Mus, dtd 23May74, hereafter *Simmons letter.*

[18] *Ibid.*

[19] Copy of Col Woods ltr to CMC filed with *Stephenson letter II.*

[20] *Stephenson letter.*

[21] *Darden interview.*

[22] Col Curtis W. LeGette Officer's Case File (Manpower Department, HQMC).

[23] *Darden interview; Hall interview.*

[24] 7th DefBn War Diaries and History, Dec40–Mar44.

[25] *Hall interview.*

[26] CMC ltr to CO, 51st DefBn, dtd 25May44, Subj: Marine Corps and Government Property, waste, misuse, pilferage, and vandalism of (Negroes in the Armed Forces File, Central Files, HQMC).

[27] Col Curtis W. LeGette ltr to CO, 51st DefBn, dtd 27Jun44, Subj: Record of the Proceedings of an Investigation Conducted at Headquarters, 51st Defense Battalion In The Field, By Order of the Commanding Officer, 51st Defense Battalion, To inquire into alleged damages to Marine Corps and Government Property formerly on charge to the 51st Defense Battalion, U. S. Marine Corps (Negroes in the Armed Forces File, Central Files, HQMC).

[28] *Stephenson letter.*

[29] FMF Status Report, Ground, dtd 31Aug44 (RefSec, Hist&MusDiv, HQMC).

[30] Commandant Samoan Defense Group ltr to Col Wade LeGette, dtd 14Aug44, in LeGette Officer's Case File, *op. cit.*

[31] *Darden interview.*

[32] *Simmons letter.*

[33] 10th AAA Bn War Diaries, May–Nov44.

[34] *Darden interview; Hall interview.*

[35] *Darden interview.*

[36] *Hall interview.*

[37] Harry McAlpin in the Baltimore *Afro-American*, 20Oct45 (Negro Marines, Press Clippings File, RefSec, Hist&MusDiv, HQMC).

Chapter 3—The 52d Defense Battalion

Unless otherwise noted, the material in this chapter is derived from: Muster rolls of the 52d Defense Battalion, Dec43—Apr46; 52d Defense Battalion War Diary, Dec43—Mar46; Detachment A, 52d Defense Battalion War Diary, Sep44—Apr45; G. H. Johnson interview; A. Johnson interview; "Montford Musings" and "52d Defense Bn." columns in *Camp Lejeune Globe*, Jan—Aug44.

[1] Col Augustus W. Cockrell Officer's Case File (Manpower Department, HQMC).

[2] BGen Joseph W. Earnshaw official biography (RefSet, Hist&MusDiv, HQMC).

[3] Col Thomas C. Moore, Jr. Officer's Case File (Manpower Department, HQMC).

[4] *A. Johnson interview.*

[5] Henry I. Shaw, Jr., Bernard T. Nalty, and Edwin T. Turnbladh, *Central Pacific Drive—History of U. S. Marine Corps Operations in World War II*, Vol. III (Washington: Historical Branch, G-3 Division, HQMC, 1966), p. 622.

[6] George W. Garand and Truman R. Strobridge, *Western Pacific Operations—History of U. S. Marine Corps Operations in World War II*, Vol. IV (Washington: Historical Division, HQMC, 1971), pp. 414–415.

[7] *A. Johnson interview.*

[8] Col David W. Silvey Officer's Case File (Manpower Department, HQMC).

[9] Atoll Commander, USNAB Navy 234 ltr to Commanding Officer, 52d Defense Battalion, dtd 7Mar45, in Col Moore's Officer's Case File, *op. cit.*

[10] *G. H. Johnson interview.*

[11] HQMC printout of all Negro battle casualties, dtd 9Apr48 (File 85A Negro Strength, RefSec, Hist&MusDiv, HQMC).

[12] "Negro Marines in World War II" typescript history written about 1946 (RefSec, Hist&MusDiv, HQMC), hereafter *Negro Marines in World War II.*

[13] *G. H. Johnson interview.*

[14] John H. Griffin "My Life in the Marine Corps" unpublished MS (Personal Paper's Collection, Museums Branch, Hist&MusDiv, HQMC)

[15] *G. H. Johnson interview.*

[16] *A. Johnson interview.*

[17] Muster rolls of Heavy Antiaircraft Group (Provisional), Saipan, Feb46-Feb47.

[18] Muster rolls of 3d Antiaircraft Artillery Battalion (Composite), May46-May47.

[19] Commanding Officer, 52d Defense Battalion ltr to CMC, dtd 15Jan46, subj: Employment of Colored Personnel as Anti-aircraft Artillery Troops; recommendations on (Personnel, Colored 1946–1948 File, Central Files, HQMC).

Chapter 4—Depot and Ammunition Companies

Unless otherwise noted, the material in this chapter is derived from: Muster Rolls of the depot and ammunition companies formed at Montford Point 1943–1946; Muster Rolls of FMF headquarters units having Stewards' Branch personnel assigned, 1944–1945; Statistics Division, Personnel Department, HQMC printout of all Negro battle casualties, dtd 9 April 1948 (File 85A, Negro Strength, RefSec, Hist&MusDiv, HQMC); Casualty cards of Negro casualties (RefSec, Hist&MusDiv, HQMC); *Huff interview;* Mr. Robert D. Little interview with HistDiv, dtd 16Aug72 (Oral History Collection, Hist&MusDiv, HQMC); Mr. Norman Sneed interview with HistDiv, dtd 16Aug72 (Oral History Collection, Hist&MusDiv, HQMC).

[1] Machine Records Section, Personnel Department, HQMC, Negro Casualties of World War II, ca. 29Jun48 (File 85A, Negro Strength, RefSec, Hist&MusDiv, HQMC).

[2] T/O D-701, Depot Company, approved 18Feb43 (RefSec, Hist&MusDiv, HQMC).

[3] Letter of Instruction 421, dtd 14May43.

[4] *Simmons letter.*

[5] T/O E-703, Ammunition Company, approved 31Aug43 (RefSec, Hist&MusDiv, HQMC).

[6] Little interview, *op. cit.*

[7] T/O E-701, Depot Company, approved 19Jul43 (RefSec, Hist&MusDiv, HQMC).

[8] *Huff interview.*

[9] *San Diego Chevron,* dtd 10Apr43 (Negro Marines Press Clippings, RefSec, Hist&MusDiv, HQMC).

[10] 4th Base Depot War Diaries and Organizational History, Apr43–Jan44.

[11] 1st Base (Field) Depot History, Mar41–Jun44, p. 4.

[12] Sneed interview, *op. cit.*; 4th Base Depot War Diaries, *op. cit.*

[13] Quoted in Capt Elmer Wilde, "Night Fighters," Marine Corps press release (Negro Marines Press Releases, RefSec, Hist&MusDiv, HQMC).

[14] Quoted in 1stSgt David M. Davies, "Officers Pleased with Performance of Race Fighters," Atlanta *Daily World,* 27Aug44 (Negro Marines Press Clippings, RefSec, Hist&MusDiv, HQMC).

[15] Quoted in "Negro Marines Win Battle Spurs; Defeated Japan's Best on Saipan," *Pittsburgh Courier,* 2Sep44 (Negro Marines Press Clippings, RefSec, Hist&MusDiv, HQMC).

[16] *Ibid.*

[17] Quoted in *Camp Lejeune Globe,* 6Jan45.

[18] *Time,* 24Jul44.

[19] Copy of ltr of commendation filed with card files for 4th Ammunition Company (RefSec, Hist&MusDiv, HQMC).

[20] 5th Field Depot War Diary, Jan45 and Apr45; Copy of Silver Star Citation, PFC Luther Woodward.

[21] Copies of citations filed with card files for 7th Ammunition Company and 11th Depot Company (RefSec, Hist&MusDiv, HQMC).

[22] George W. Garand and Truman R. Strobridge, *Western Pacific Operations—History of U. S. Marine Corps Operations in World War II,* Vol. IV (Washington: HistDiv, HQMC, 1971), pp. 708—10.

[23] Muster Roll, 36th Marine Depot Company, Aug45; Montford Point Marine Association Convention Program, Aug72, p. 10.

[24] Garand and Strobridge, *op. cit.,* p. 710.

[25] USS *Bladen* (APA-63) Action Report, Serial 08 of 14Apr45 (Operational Archives Branch, Naval Historical Center).

[26] Unless otherwise noted the material on the occupation of Japan and North China is derived from: Henry I. Shaw, Jr. *The United States Marines in the Occupation of Japan* and *The United States Marines in North China, 1945–1949* (Washington: HistBr, G–3 Div, HQMC, 1969 and 1968).

[27] *Huff interview.*

[28] Information regarding the investigation is derived from: Guam Island Commander ltr to Col Samuel A. Woods, Jr., dtd 30Dec44, Subj: Court of Inquiry to inquire into the unlawful assembly and riot and the attending circumstances at the Naval Supply Depot, Guam, on 25 and 26 December 1944, including Record of Proceedings (Navy JAG File 9/57:24–1—#35227).

[29] *Ibid.* Exhibit 2, Record of Proceedings.

[30] *Ibid.* Record of Proceedings, p. 708.

[31] Quoted in Montford Point Marine Association Convention Program, Aug72, p. 16.

[32] Little interview, *op. cit.*

Chapter 5—Between the Wars

Unless otherwise noted the material in this chapter is derived from: Muster rolls of units at Montford Point Camp, 1944–49; 85A Negro, Miscellaneous File, Personnel Department (RefSec, Hist&MusDiv, HQMC); "The History of the Negro Officer in the Marine Corps" and "Negro Marines in World War II" (Negro Press Release File RefSec, Hist&MusDiv, HQMC); G. H. Johnson interview; Huff interview; Camp Lejeune Globe, 1945–1949.

1 Selective Service System, Special Groups (Special Monograph No. 10), 2 vols. (Washington: Government Printing Office, 1953) II, pp. 201–202.

2 G–1 (M–1) Section, Division of Plans and Policies, HQMC, Operational Diarys, 7Dec41–31Aug45, Section XV, Colored Personnel (Folder 67, Administrative History File, RefSec, Hist&MusDiv, HQMC).

3 Col Augustus W. Cockrell ltr to MajGen Dewitt Peck, dtd 8Jan45 in SgtMaj Charles F. Anderson Enlisted Case File (Manpower Department, HQMC)

4 "Montford Musings," Camp Lejeune Globe, 21Mar45.

5 9th Platoon Commanders Class statistics in 1st Sgt Charles W. Simmons Enlisted Case File (Manpower Department, HQMC).

6 G. H. Johnson interview.

7 Simmons letter.

8 Officer in Charge, Statistics Division, Personnel Department memo to Director of Public Information, dtd 13Jul48 (85A Negro Miscellaneous File, Personnel Department, RefSec, Hist&MusDiv, HQMC).

9 Camp Lejeune Globe, 6Feb46.

10 Ibid., 3Jan46.

11 Darden interview; Norfolk Journal and Guide, 4May46 (Negro Press Clippings File, RefSec, Hist&MusDiv, HQMC).

12 Director, Division of Plans and Policies memo to CMC, dtd 8 Apr 46, Subj: Negro Personnel in the Post-War Marine Corps (Personnel, Colored, 1946–1948 File, Central Files, HQMC).

13 Ibid.

14 Ibid.

15 Director, Division of Plans and Policies memo to CMC, dtd 13 May 46, Subj: Negro Personnel in the Post-War Marine Corps, with subsequent memoranda (Personnel, Colored, 1946–1948 File, Central Files, HQMC).

16 Ibid.

17 Ibid.

18 Col John F. Mallard Officer's Case File (Manpower Department, HQMC).

19 Camp Lejeune Globe, 13Feb46.

20 Ibid., 29May46.

21 G. H. Johnson interview.

22 Commanding Officer, Marine Barracks, Naval Ammunition Depot, McAlester, Okla. ltr to CMC, dtd 5Nov46, Subj: Assignment of colored Marines (Personnel, Colored, 1946–1948 File, Central Files, HQMC).

23 Ibid.

24 Director, Plans and Policies memo to CMC, dtd 6Dec46, Subj: Assignment of Negro Marines to MB, Naval Magazine, Port Chicago, California, in lieu of MB, NAD, McAlester, Okla. (Personnel, Colored, 1946–1948 File, Central Files, HQMC).

25 CNO memo to CMC, dtd 6Jan47, Subj: Assignment of Negro Marines to Marine Barracks, Naval Magazine, Port Chicago, Calif., and Marine Barracks, Naval Ammunition Depot, Earle, N. J. (Personnel, Colored, 1946–1948 File, Central Files, HQMC).

26 Division of Plans and Policies memo to CMC, dtd 30Jan47, Subj: Negro requirements (Personnel, Colored, 1946–1948 File, Central Files, HQMC).

27 Commandant, 12th Naval District naval speedletter, to CMC, dtd 5Mar47 (Personnel, Colored, 1946–1948 File, Central Files, HQMC).

28 Commandant, 12th Naval District naval speedletter, to CMC, dtd 6Jun47 (Personnel, Colored, 1946–1948 File, Central Files, HQMC).

29 Division of Plans and Policies memo to CMC, dtd 29May47, Subj: Program for Accelerated Attrition of Negro Marines (Personnel, Colored, 1946–1948 File, Central Files, HQMC).

30 Division of Plans and Policies memo to CMC, dtd 28Aug47, Subj: Requirements for General Duty Negro Marines (Personnel, Colored, 1946–1948 File, Central Files, HQMC).

31 Huff interview.

32 G. H. Johnson interview.

33 Huff interview.

34 Division of Plans and Policies memo to CMC, dtd 11Jun47, Subj: Negro Requirements as Assignments (Personnel, Colored, 1946–1948 File, Central Files, HQMC).

35 CMC naval speedletter to Commandant, 12th Naval District, dtd 18Jun47 (personnel, Colored, 1946–1948 File, Central Files, HQMC).

36 CMC ltr to Commanding Officer, Marine Barracks, Naval Ammunition Depot, Hingham, Mass., dtd 18Jun47, Subj: Assignment of Negro Marines; CMC ltr to Commanding Officer, Marine Barracks, Naval Ammunition Depot, Ft. Mifflin, Pa., dtd 18Jun47 (Personnel, Colored, 1946–1948 File, Central Files, HQMC).

37 CMC ltr to Commanding Officer, Marine Barracks, Naval Shipyard, Brooklyn, N. Y., dtd 18Jun47, Subj: Assignment of Negro Marines to Second Guard Company (Personnel, Colored, 1946–1948 File, Central Files, HQMC).

38 Commanding Officer, Marine Barracks, Naval Shipyard, Brooklyn, N. Y. ltr to CMC, dtd 30Jun47 (Personnel, Colored, 1946–1948 File, Central Files, HQMC).

39 Commanding Officer, Marine Barracks, Naval Ammunition Depot, Hingham, Mass. ltr to CMC, dtd 26Jun47, Subj: Comments on Assignment of Negro Marines (Personnel, Colored, 1946–1948 File, Central Files, HQMC).

40 Commandant, Naval Base, New York, N. Y. ltr to CMC, dtd 10Jul47, Subj: Assignment of Negro Marines to Second Guard Company, Marine Barracks, New York Naval Shipyard, Brooklyn, N. Y. (Personnel, Colored, 1946–1948 File, Central Files, HQMC).

41 Division of Plans and Policies memo to CMC, dtd 29Jul47, Subj: Negro Requirements and Assignments (Personnel, Colored, 1946–1948 File, Central Files, HQMC).

42 Bureau of Ordnance memo to CNO (Op–04), dtd 11Aug47, Subj: Naval Ammunition Depot, Earle, N. J.; Assignment of Negro Marine Complement (Personnel Colored, 1946–1948 File, Central Files, HQMC).

43 Division of Plans and Policies memo to CMC, dtd 20Aug47, Subj: Assignments of Negro Marines (Personnel, Colored, 1946–1948 File, Central Files, HQMC).

44 Division of Plans and Policies memo to CMC, dtd 28Aug47, Subj: Requirements for General Duty Marines (Personnel, Colored, 1946–1948 File, Central Files, HQMC).

[45] Bureau of Supplies and Accounts memo to CNO, dtd 14Oct47, Subj: Assignment of Negro Marines (Personnel, Colored, 1946–1948 File, Central Files, HQMC).

[46] Division of Plans and Policies memo to CMC, dtd 19Nov47 (Personnel Colored, 1946–1948 File, Central Files, HQMC).

[47] CNO memo to Chief, Bureau of Ordnance, dtd 6Jan48, Subj: Assignment of Negro Marines at Naval Ammunition Depot, Earle, Red Bank, New Jersey (Personnel, Colored, 1946–1948 File, Central Files, HQMC).

[48] Richard J. Stillman, II, *Integration of the Negro in the U. S. Armed Forces* (New York: Frederick A. Praeger, 1968), pp. 37–38.

[49] 1948 *Facts on File*, p. 96.

[50] Stillman, *op. cit.*, p. 38.

[51] SgtMaj Gilbert H. Johnson Enlisted Case File (Manpower Department, HQMC).

[52] 1948 *Facts on File*, p. 244J-K.

[53] Stillman, *op. cit.*, p. 44.

[54] *Time*, 5Jun50.

[55] CMC memo to Assistant Secretary of the Navy (Air), dtd 17Mar49 (1535–110 Negroes-Asiatic, 1Jan49–30Jun50 File, Central Files, HQMC).

[56] 1949 *Facts on File*, p. 133P.

[57] ALNAV 49–447, dtd 23Jun49 in *Navy Department Bulletin*, Jan-Jun 1949, p. 38.

[58] Marine Corps memo, dtd 18Nov49 (1535–110 Negroes-Asiatic, 1Jan49–30Jun30 File, Central Files, HQMC).

[59] *Camp Lejeune Globe*, 27Feb46.

[60] Division of Plans and Policies memo to CMC, dtd 14Feb46, Subj: Letter of Instruction 421: revocation of (Negro Marines, 1946–1948 File, Central Files, HQMC).

[61] Gen Alfred H. Noble interview by HistDiv, HQMC, dtd 20–23May68 (Oral History Collection, Hist&MusDiv, HQMC), p. 103.

[62] *Chicago Defender*, 19Feb49 (Negro Press Clippings File, RefSec, Hist&MusDiv, HQMC).

[63] *Ibid.*

[64] LtCol Pat Meid, USMCR, *Marine Corps Women's Reserve In World War II* (Washington: HistBr, G-3 Div, HQMC, 1968), p. 94.

[65] Mr. A. Philip Randolph ltr to Gen Clifton B. Cates, dtd 8May49 (1535–110 Negroes-Asiatics, 1Jan49–30Jun 50 File, Central Files, HQMC).

[66] Gen Clifton B. Cates ltr to Mr. Philip Randolph, dtd 10Mar49 (1535–110Negroes-Asiatics, 1Jan49–30Jun50 File, Central Files, HQMC).

[67] LtCol Frank W. Ferguson Officer's Case File (Manpower Department, HQMC).

[68] *Huff interview.*

[69] *G. H. Johnson interview.*

Chapter 6—A Decade of Integration

Unless otherwise noted the material in this chapter is derived from: 85A Negro Miscellaneous File, Personnel Department (RefSec, Hist&MusDiv, HQMC): "The History of the Negro Officer in the Marine Corps" (Negro Press Release File, RefSec, Hist&MusDiv, HQMC); G. H. Johnson interview; Huff interview; CWO James E. Johnson interview with Historical Division, dated 27Mar73 and 30Oct73 (Oral History Collection, Hist&MusDiv, HQMC). hereafter J. E. Johnson interview; LtCol Frank Petersen, Jr. interview with Historical Division, HQMC, dtd 1Aug72 (Oral History Collection, Hist&Mus Div, HQMC), hereafter Petersen interview.

1 85A Negro Strength 46–53 File (RefSec, Hist&MusDiv, HQMC).

2 Office of the Assistant Secretary of Defense (Comptroller), Directorate of Information Operations, Selected Manpower Statistics (Washington, 15 April 1971), p. 19.

3 Ibid.; 85A Negro Strength 46–53 File (RefSec, Hist&Mus Div, HQMC).

4 Washington Post, 27Feb51 (Negro Marine Press Clippings 1950's File, RefSec, Hist&Mus Div, HQMC), HQMC).

5 LtGen Homer A. Litzenberg, Jr. official biography (RefSec, Hist&Mus Div, HQMC).

6 Gen Oliver P. Smith interview by Oral History Unit, Historical Div, HQMC, dtd 9–11–22Jun69 (Oral History Collection, Hist&MusDiv, HQMC).

7 Race Data Reporting File 53–54 (RefSec, Hist&Mus Div, HQMC).

8 1535–110, Negroes-Asiatics, 1Jan49-30June50 File (Central Files, HQMC.)

9 Cpl Donald Woody casualty card (Casualty Files, Korean War, RefSec, Hist&MusDiv, HQMC).

10 Daily Northwestern, 4Nov52 (Negro Marine Press Clippings 1950s File RefSec, Hist&MusDiv, HQMC).

11 Ibid.

12 PFC A C Clark Silver Star Citation (Manpower Department, HQMC).

13 Ibid.; PFC A C Clark Bronze Star Citation (Manpower Department, HQMC).

14 Huff interview.

15 Ibid.

16 85A Negro Personnel 1952 File (RefSec, Hist&MusDiv, HQMC).

17 G. H. Johnson interview.

18 LtCol Frank E. Petersen, Jr. Officer's Case File (Manpower Department, HQMC); Petersen interview.

19 LtCol Kenneth H. Berthoud, Jr. Officer's Case File (Manpower Department, HQMC).

20 LtCol Hurdle L. Maxwell official biography (RefSec, Hist&MusDiv, HQMC).

21 Huff interview; HQMC, Listing of Retired Marine Corps Personnel (NAVMC 1005C) (Washington, 9May73).

22 Huff interview.

23 Col Harlan C. Cooper official biography (RefSec, Hist&MusDiv, HQMC).

24 Manpower Statistics, op. cit., p. 23

25 J. E. Johnson interview; LtGen Joseph C. Burger interview by Oral History Unit, Historical Division, HQMC, dtd 2Dec69 (Oral History Collection, Hist&MusDiv, HQMC).

26 J. E. Johnson interview.

27 1954 FOF, p. 221B2.

28 Burger interview, op. cit.

29 J. E. Johnson interview.

30 1954 FOF, p. 163C1.

31 1954 FOF, p. 38B1.

32 1955 FOF, p. 369C2 and 1956, p. 380B1.

33 1957 FOF, 284D3 –285B1 and 1960, p. 124A1.

Chapter 7—The Vietnam Era

Unless otherwise noted the material in this section is derived from: Senior Member, Inquiry Team memo 2/3: JRL: rfc-3000 to Commanding General, Marine Corps Base, Camp Smedley D. Butler, dtd 4Oct71, Subj: Report of Racial Turbulence Inquiry (CMC Letter Files, RefSec, Hist&MusDiv, HQMC); Negro Marines Civil Rights, Equal Opportunity Reports, and Race Relations Files (RefSec. Hist&MusDiv HQMC); *Huff interview; Petersen interview;* President's Committee on Equal Opportunity in the Armed Forces, *Equality of Treatment and Opportunity for Negro Military Personnel Stationed within the United States* (Washington: Government Printing Office, 13Jun63), hereafter *Gesell Report.*

1 1961 *FOF*, p. 379A-B3.
2 Special Assistant for Minority Affairs comments on draft manuscript, "A Brief History of Blacks in the Marine Corps," n.d. (ca. Sep74).
3 *Ibid.*
4 *Ibid.*
5 Assistant Secretary of Defense memo to Undersecretaries of Army, Navy, and Air Force, dtd 7May62 (Negro Marines Civil Rights File. RefSec, Hist&MusDiv. HQMC).
6 AOIC memo for the record, dtd 18Jul62, Subj: Meeting with Civil Rights Commission Representative (Negro Marines Civil Rights File. RefSec. Hist&MusDiv, HQMC).
7 *Gesell Report*, p. 48
8 *Ibid.*
9 *Ibid.*, p. 75.
10 Mayor A. D. Guy ltr to MajGen Alpha L. Bowser, dtd 14Aug63 (LtGen James P. Berkeley papers, Manuscript Collection, Hist&MusDiv, HQMC).
11 MajGen Alpha L. Bowser ltr to LtGen James P. Berkeley, dtd 23Aug63 (LtGen James P. Berkeley papers, Manuscript Collection, Hist&MusDiv. HQMC).
12 DoD Directive 5120.36, dtd 26Jul63, Subj: Equal Opportunity in the Armed Forces (Negro Marines Equal Opportunity Reports File. RefSec, Hist&MusDiv, HQMC).
13 1967 *FOF*, p. 536A-E2
14 Director of Information ltr to Assistant Chief of Staff, G-1, dtd 26Dec63, Subj: Equal Opportunity Report (Negro Marines Equal Opportunity Reports File, RefSec, Hist&MusDiv, HQMC).
15 Secretary of the Navy ALNAV, dtd 9Jul64, Subj: DOD Policy Regarding NavDept Participation (Negro Marines—Equal Opportunity Reports File, RefSec, Hist&MusDiv, HQMC).
16 *Selections from the Report of the National Commission on Civil Disorders* (New York: Scholastic Book Services, 1969), p. 18.
17 *Ibid*, p. 19.
18 Equal Opportunity Branch, Summary of Significant Racial Incidents at Major Marine Corps Installations, August 1968—November 1971 (Negro Marines Race Relations File, RefSec, Hist&MusDiv, HQMC).
19 House Armed Services Committee, *Inquiry into the Disturbances at Marine Corps Base, Camp Lejeune, N.C., on July 20, 1969* (Washington, 15Dec69), p. 5053, hereafter *HASC Inquiry.*
20 *Ibid.*, p. 5054.
21 Copy in Negro Marines Race Relations File, RefSec, Hist&MusDiv, HQMC.
22 *HASC Inquiry,* p. 5051-5052.
23 *Ibid.*, pp. 5053-5054.

24 Summary of Racial Incidents, *op. cit.*, p. 2; 1970 *FOF*, p. 245G1.
25 *HASC Inquiry*, p. 5051-5052.
26 *Ibid.*, p. 5059.
27 *Washington Post*, 16Aug69, p. A-5.
28 USMC News Release No. 179-69, CMC Press Conference at the Pentagon, dtd 3Sep69 (Negro Marines Press Release File. RefSec, Hist&Mus Div, HQMC).
29 Copy in Negro Marines Race Relations File, RefSec. Hist&MusDiv, HQMC.
30 *USMC News Release* No. 179—69, *op. cit,*
31 Department of Defense, *Commanders Digest*, v. 6, no. 24 (13Sep69), pp. 1, 7.
32 Additional sources for this section include: HQMC Staff Report of Major Accomplishments, FY 72, Book 2 (G-1 Div), Tab 13, "CMC Advisory Committee for Minority Affairs," dtd 11Dec72, hereafter *Advisory Committee* and Tab 14, "Marine Corps Human Relations Institute," dtd 11Dec72, hereafter *Human Relations Institute;* Chief of Staff Project 23-67, dtd 10Feb69, hereafter *CofS Project 23-67* (RefSec, Hist&Mus Div, HQMC).
33 *CofS Project 23-67*; Department of Defense (Comptroller), Directorate for Information Operations, *Selected Manpower Statistics* (Washington, 15Apr71), p. 24.
34 Director of Information memo to Director of Marine Corps History and Museums, dtd 19Jul74, Subj: "A Brief History of Blacks in the Marine Corps." (Comment File, RefSec. Hist&MusDiv, HQMC).
35 "A Special Tribute to the Founders of the Montford Point Marine Association," in 1972 Program of the Montford Point Marine Association Annual Convention (Negro Marines, Publications File. RefSec. Hist&MusDiv, HQMC).
36 Interview with Maj Edward L. Green in *Pittsburg Courier*, 7Oct72 (Negro Marines Press Clippings File, RefSec, Hist&MusDiv HQMC).
37 *Ibid.*
38 Head, Equal Opportunity Branch memo MPE-23-jj to Head, Histories Section, dtd 7Dec73, Subj: Composition of Black Officers and Enlisted Grades by Sex as of 30 September 1973 (Negro Marines Statistics File. RefSec, Hist&MusDiv HQMC).
39 *Ibid.*
40 *San Diego Union*, 18Sep71 (Negro Marines Press Clippings File, RefSec, Hist&MusDiv, HQMC).
41 Equal Opportunity Branch, Mission and Functions Statement (Negro Marines, Equal Opportunity Branch, 1969 File, RefSec, Hist&MusDiv HQMC).
42 Quoted in *CofS Project 23-67.*
43 Office of the Assistant Secretary of Defense (Public Affairs) News Release No. 307-73, dtd 21Jun73 (Negro Marines News Release File, RefSec, Hist&MusDiv HQMC).
44 HQMC Staff Report of Major Accomplishments, 1970-1971, Book 22 (G-1 Div), Tab 17 (RefSec, Hist&MusDiv, HQMC).
45 *Advisory Committee.*
46 *Ibid.*
47 HQMC News Release No. KTW-230-71, General McCutcheon's CG's OP (Negro Marines News Release File, RefSec, Hist&MusDiv, HQMC).
48 *A Brief History of the III Marine Amphibious Force* (Historical Division, September 1971); BGen Edwin H. Sim-

mons, "Marine Corps Operations in Vietnam, 1969–1972," *U.S. Naval Institute Proceedings*, v. 99, no. 843 (May 1973).

[49] Information provided by Manpower Planning, Programs, and Policy Branch, HQMC on 25 February 1974.

[50] LtCol Frank E. Petersen, Jr. Officer's Case File (Manpower Department, HQMC).

[51] SgtMaj Edgar R. Huff Enlisted Case File (Manpower Department, HQMC).

[52] Capt Moyers S. Shore, *The Battle for Khe Sanh* (Washington: Historical Branch, G–3 Division, HQMC, 1969), p. 145.

[53] SgtMaj Agrippa W. Smith Enlisted Case File (Manpower Department, HQMC).

[54] Individual Citations and Background Data (Medal of Honor file, RefSec, Hist&MusDiv HQMC).

[55] *Chicago Daily Defender*, 27Jul71, citing remarks by BGen Robert D. Bohn, USMC in an article in the August 1971 issue of *Sepia* (Negro Marines Press Clippings File, RefSec, Hist&MusDiv HQMC).

[56] *Ibid.*

[57] *G. H. Johnson interview.*

[58] *Huff interview.*

[59] Program of the Camp Lejeune Chapter, Montford Point Marine Association, Fourth Annual Testimonial Dinner Honoring The Honorable Howard N. Lee, Mayor, Chapel Hill, N.C. (Negro Marines, Publications File, RefSec, Hist&MusDiv HQMC).

[60] Assistant Secretary of the Navy (Manpower and Reserve Affairs) ltr to Mr. Grant T. Hallmon, dtd 10Oct73 (Negro Marines Interview Back-up File, RefSec, Hist&MusDiv, HQMC).

[61] *Camp Lejeune Globe*, 25Apr74

APPENDIX B

BLACK MARINE UNITS
OF THE FLEET MARINE FORCE, WORLD WAR II

Date of Activation	Unit Designation	Date of Deactivation	Where Deactivated
18 Aug 1942	51st Composite Def Bn	31 Jan 1946	Montford Point
8 Mar 1943	1st Marine Depot Co	4 Jan 1946	Montford Point
23 Apr 1943	2d Marine Depot Co	4 Jan 1946	Montford Point
23 Apr 1943	3d Marine Depot Co	4 Jan 1946	Montford Point
1 June 1943	4th Marine Depot Co	31 Oct 1945	Guam
8 Jul 1943	5th Marine Depot Co	31 Oct 1943	New Caledonia
8 Jul 1943	6th Marine Depot Co	31 Aug 1943	New Caledonia
16 Aug 1943	7th Marine Depot Co	11 Dec 1945	Montford Point
16 Aug 1943	8th Marine Depot Co	10 Dec 1945	Montford Point
15 Sep 1943	9th Marine Depot Co	31 Dec 1945	Montford Point
15 Sep 1943	10th Marine Depot Co	22 Dec 1945	Montford Point
1 Oct 1943	1st Marine Ammunition Co	21 Feb 1946	Montford Point
7 Oct 1943	11th Marine Depot Co	4 Dec 1945	Saipan
7 Oct 1943	12th Marine Depot Co	11 Dec 1945	Montford Point
1 Nov 1943	13th Marine Depot Co	30 Nov 1945	Guam
1 Nov 1943	14th Marine Depot Co	30 Nov 1945	Guam
1 Nov 1943	2d Marine Ammunition Co	20 Jan 1946	Guam
1 Dec 1943	15th Marine Depot Co	30 Nov 1945	Allen Island
2 Dec 1943	16th Marine Depot Co	29 Jan 1946	Montford Point
2 Dec 1943	3d Marine Ammunition Co	25 Feb 1946	Montford Point
15 Dec 1943	52d Defense Bn	14 May 1946	Montford Point
1 Jan 1944	17th Marine Depot Co	16 Jan 1946	Montford Point
1 Jan 1944	18th Marine Depot Co	29 Jan 1946	Montford Point
1 Jan 1944	4th Marine Ammunition Co	8 Mar 1946	Guam
1 Feb 1944	19th Marine Depot Co	25 Feb 1946	Montford Point
1 Feb 1944	20th Marine Depot Co	21 Feb 1946	Montford Point
1 Feb 1944	5th Marine Ammunition Co	4 Jul 1946	Montford Point
1 Mar 1944	21st Marine Depot Co	2 Apr 1946	Montford Point
1 Mar 1944	22d Marine Depot Co	2 Apr 1946	Montford Point
1 Mar 1944	6th Ammunition Co	15 Dec 1945	Sasebo
1 Apr 1944	23d Marine Depot Co	5 Apr 1946	Montford Point
1 Apr 1944	24th Marine Depot Co	15 Nov 1945	Nagasaki
1 Apr 1944	7th Marine Ammunition Co	8 May 1946	Montford Point
1 May 1944	25th Marine Depot Co	2 May 1946	Montford Point
1 May 1944	26th Marine Depot Co	2 May 1946	Montford Point
1 May 1944	8th Marine Ammunition Co	30 Sep 1947	Guam
1 Jun 1944	27th Marine Depot Co	16 Apr 1946	Montford Point
1 Jun 1944	28th Marine Depot Co	2 May 1946	Montford Point
1 Jun 1944	9th Marine Ammunition Co	4 Jul 1946	Montford Point
1 Jul 1944	29th Marine Depot Co	8 May 1946	Montford Point
1 Jul 1944	30th Marine Depot Co	8 Apr 1946	Montford Point
1 Jul 1944	10th Marine Ammunition Co	6 May 1946	Montford Point
1 Aug 1944	31st Marine Depot Co	30 Nov 1945	Maui
1 Aug 1944	32d Marine Depot Co	8 May 1946	Montford Point
1 Aug 1944	11th Marine Ammunition Co	4 Jul 1946	Montford Point
1 Sep 1944	33d Marine Depot Co	31 Jan 1946	Guam
1 Sep 1944	34th Marine Depot Co	31 Jan 1946	Guam
1 Sep 1944	12th Marine Ammunition Co	5 Apr 1946	Montford Point
1 Oct 1944	35th Marine Depot Co	6 Jun 1946	Montford Point
1 Oct 1944	36th Marine Depot Co	17 Jun 1946	Montford Point
1 Nov 1944	37th Marine Depot Co	2 Apr 1946	Montford Point
1 Nov 1944	38th Marine Depot Co	2 Apr 1946	Montford Point

Date of Activation	Unit Designation	Date of Deactivation	Where Deactivated
1 Nov 1944	5th Marine Depot Co	21 Feb 1946	Montford Point
1 Dec 1944	6th Marine Depot Co	31 Dec 1945	Guam
1 Dec 1944	39th Marine Depot Co	10 Jun 1946	Guam
1 Dec 1944	40th Marine Depot Co	4 May 1946	Saipan
3 Mar 1945	41st Marine Depot Co	23 Mar 1946	Maui
14 Mar 1945	42d Marine Depot Co	15 Mar 1946	Sasebo
14 Mar 1945	43d Marine Depot Co	15 Mar 1946	Sasebo
18 Apr 1945	44th Marine Depot Co	8 Apr 1946	Montford Point
10 Aug 1945	45th Marine Depot Co	6 Jun 1946	Montford Point
1 Oct 1945	46th Marine Depot Co	15 Jul 1946	Montford Point
1 Oct 1945	47th Marine Depot Co	31 Oct 1946	Oahu
1 Oct 1945	48th Marine Depot Co	10 Jun 1946	Guam
1 Oct 1945	49th Marine Depot Co	30 Sep 1947	Guam

APPENDIX C

BLACK MARINE MEDAL OF HONOR RECIPIENTS

The President of the United States in the name of the Congress takes pride in presenting the
MEDAL OF HONOR posthumously to

PRIVATE FIRST CLASS JAMES ANDERSON, JR
UNITED STATES MARINE CORPS

for service as set forth in the following
CITATION:

For conspicuous gallantry and intrepidity at the risk of his life above and beyond the call of duty as a rifleman, Second Platoon, Company F, Second Battalion, Third Marines, Third Marine Division in Vietnam on 28 February 1967. Company F was advancing in dense jungle northwest of Cam Lo in an effort to extract a heavily besieged reconnaissance patrol. Private First Class Anderson's platoon was the lead element and had advanced only about 200 meters when they were brought under extremely intense enemy small arms and automatic weapons fire. Private First Class Anderson found himself tightly bunched together with the other members of the platoon only 20 meters from the enemy positions. As the fire fight continued several of the men were wounded by the deadly enemy assault. Suddenly, an enemy grenade landed in the midst of the Marines and rolled along side Private First Class Anderson's head. Unhesitatingly and with complete disregard for his own personal safety, he reached out, grasped the grenade, pulled it to his chest and curled around it as it went off. Although several Marines received shrapnel from the grenade, his body absorbed the major force of the explosion. In this singularly heroic act, Private First Class Anderson saved his comrades from serious injury and possible death. His personal heroism, extraordinary valor, and inspirational supreme self-sacrifice reflected great credit upon himself and the Marine Corps and upheld the highest traditions of the United States Naval Service. He gallantly gave his life for his country.

Private First Class James Anderson Jr., Medal of Honor Recipient (Posthumous) (USMC Photo A417058).

97

The President of the United States in the name of the Congress takes pride in presenting the
MEDAL OF HONOR posthumously to

SERGEANT RODNEY M. DAVIS
UNITED STATES MARINE CORPS

for service as set forth in the following
CITATION:

For conspicuous gallantry and intrepidity at the risk of his life above and beyond the call of duty while serving as the right guide of the Second Platoon, Company B, First Battalion, Fifth Marines, First Marine Division, in action against enemy forces in Quang Nam Province, Republic of Vietnam, on 6 September 1967. Elements of the Second Platoon were pinned down by a numerically superior force of attacking North Vietnamese Army Regulars. Remnants of the platoon were located in a trench line where Sergeant Davis was directing the fire of his men in an attempt to repel the enemy attack. Disregarding the enemy hand grenades and high volume of small arms and mortar fire, Sergeant Davis moved from man to man shouting words of encouragement to each of them while firing and throwing grenades at the onrushing enemy. When an enemy grenade landed in the trench in the midst of his men, Sergeant Davis, realizing the gravity of the situation, and in a final valiant act of complete self-sacrifice, instantly threw himself upon the grenade, absorbing with his own body the full and terrific force of the explosion. Through his extraordinary initiative and inspiring valor in the face of almost certain death, Sergeant Davis saved his comrades from injury and possible loss of life, enabled his platoon to hold its vital position, and upheld the highest traditions of the Marine Corps and the United States Naval Service. He gallantly gave his life for his country.

Sergeant Rodney M. Davis, Medal of Honor Recipient (Posthumous). (USMC Photo A417499).

The President of the United States in the name of the Congress takes pride in presenting the MEDAL OF HONOR posthumously to

PRIVATE FIRST CLASS RALPH H. JOHNSON
UNITED STATES MARINE CORPS

For service as set forth in the following

CITATION:

For conspicuous gallantry and intrepidity at the risk of his life above and beyond the call of duty while serving as a Reconnaissance Scout with Company A, First Reconnaissance Battalion, First Marine Division in action against the North Vietnamese Army and Viet Cong Forces in the Republic of Vietnam. In the early morning hours of 5 March 1968, during Operation ROCK, Private First Class Johnson was a member of a fifteen-man reconnaissance patrol manning an observation post on Hill 146 overlooking the Quan Duc Duc Valley deep in enemy controlled territory. They were attacked by a platoon-size hostile force employing automatic weapons, satchel charges and hand grenades. Suddenly, a hand grenade landed in the three-man fighting hole occupied by Private Johnson and two fellow marines. Realizing the inherent danger to his two comrades, he shouted a warning and unhesitatingly hurled himself upon the explosive device. When the grenade exploded, Private Johnson absorbed the tremendous impact of the blast and was killed instantly. His prompt and heroic act saved the life of one marine at the cost of his own and undoubtedly prevented the enemy from penetrating his sector of the patrol's perimeter. Private Johnson's courage, inspiring valor and selfless devotion to duty were in keeping with the highest traditions of the Marine Corps and the United States Naval Service. He gallantly gave his life for his country.

Private First Class Ralph H. Johnson, Medal of Honor Recipient (Posthumous). (USMC Photo A700430).

The President of the United States in the name of The Congress takes pride in presenting the MEDAL OF HONOR posthumously to

PRIVATE FIRST CLASS OSCAR P. AUSTIN
UNITED STATES MARINE CORPS

for service as set forth in the following

CITATION:

For conspicuous gallantry and intrepidity at the risk of his life above and beyond the call of duty serving as an Assistant Machine Gunner with Company E, Second Battalion, Seventh Marines, First Marine Division in connection with operations against enemy forces in the Republic of Vietnam. During the early morning hours of 23 February 1969, Private First Class Austin's observation post was subjected to a fierce ground attack by a large North Vietnamese Army force supported by a heavy volume of hand grenades, satchel charges and small arms fire. Observing that one of his wounded companions had fallen unconscious in a position dangerously exposed to the hostile fire, Private First Class Austin unhesitatingly left the relative security of his fighting hole and, with complete disregard for his own safety, raced across the fire-swept terrain to assist the Marine to a covered location. As he neared the casualty, he observed an enemy grenade land nearby and, reacting instantly, leaped between the injured Marine and the lethal object, absorbing the effects of its detonation. As he ignored his painful injuries and turned to examine the wounded man, he saw a North Vietnamese Army soldier aiming a weapon at his unconscious companion. With full knowledge of the probable consequences and thinking only to protect the Marine, Private First Class Austin resolutely threw himself between the casualty and the hostile soldier and, in so doing, was mortally wounded. Private First Class Austin's indomitable courage, inspiring initiative and selfless devotion to duty upheld the highest traditions of the Marine Corps and the United States Naval Service. He gallantly gave his life for his country.

Private First Class Oscar P. Austin, Medal of Honor Recipient
(Posthumous) (USMC Photo A700428)

The President of the United States in the name of the Congress takes pride in presenting the MEDAL OF HONOR posthumously to

PRIVATE FIRST CLASS ROBERT H. JENKINS, JR.
UNITED STATES MARINE CORPS

for service as set forth in the following
CITATION

For conspicuous gallantry and intrepidity at the risk of his life above and beyond the call of duty while serving as a Machine Gunner with Company C, Third Reconnaissance Battalion, Third Marine Division in connection with operations against enemy forces in the Republic of Vietnam. Early on the morning of 5 March 1969, Private First Class Jenkins' twelve-man reconnaissance team was occupying a defensive position at Fire Support Base Argonne south of the Demilitarized Zone. Suddenly, the Marines were assaulted by a North Vietnamese Army platoon employing mortars, automatic weapons, and hand grenades. Reacting instantly, Private First Class Jenkins and another Marine quickly moved into a two-man fighting emplacement, and as they boldly delivered accurate machine gun fire against the enemy, a North Vietnamese soldier threw a hand grenade into the friendly emplacement. Fully realizing the inevitable results of his actions, Private First Class Jenkins quickly seized his comrade, and pushing the man to the ground, he leaped on top of the Marine to shield him from the explosion. Absorbing the full impact of the detonation, Private First Class Jenkins was seriously injured and subsequently succumbed to his wounds. His courage, inspiring valor and selfless devotion to duty saved a fellow Marine from serious injury or possible death and upheld the highest traditions of the Marine Corps and the United States Naval Service. He gallantly gave his life for his country.

Private First Class Robert H. Jenkins, Medal of Honor Recipient (Posthumous). (USMC Photo A700433).

INDEX

☆U.S. GOVERNMENT PRINTING OFFICE: 1976 O—592-056

The device reproduced on the back cover is the oldest military insignia in continuous use in the United States. It first appeared, as shown here, on Marine Corps buttons adapted in 1804. With the stars changed to five points this device has continued on Marine Corps buttons to the present day.

www.ingramcontent.com/pod-product-compliance
Lightning Source LLC
Chambersburg PA
CBHW080518110426
42742CB00017B/3159